REVISED EDITION

The Smithsonian Collection of
CLASSIC JAZZ

Selected and annotated by
Martin Williams

with a biographical index by Ira Gitler

93-2044   The Smithsonian Collection of Recordings
Washington DC
1987

The Smithsonian Collection of Recordings
is a division of the Smithsonian Institution Press,
Felix C. Lowe, *Director.*

Executive Producer: J.R. Taylor
Associate Producer: Margaret Robinson
Editorial and Design Director: Jane Sapp
Business Manager: Judie Gumbita
Financial Manager, SI Press: John Ouellette
Marketing Manager: Margaret Kei Mooney

Album Producer: Margaret Robinson
Mastering Engineer: Jack Towers
Booklet Editor: Jane Sapp
Research Assistant: Elizabeth Eaton
Production Assistant: Kate Adams
Graphic Designer: Christopher Jones

We are grateful for the use of source recordings supplied by George Hall, Jim Lyons, Dan Morgenstern, David Rossen, Jan Rossen, Phil Schaap, Jack Towers, the Institute of Jazz Studies, and the participating record companies.

Special thanks for information, help, and advice from Edward Berger, Thomas Cunniffe, Stanley Dance, James Dapogny, Nesuhi Ertegun, Julian Euell, Ira Gitler, Ralph J. Gleason, Mark Gridley, John Hammond, Larry Kart, Dick Katz, Lee Konitz, Gus Matzorkis, Don Miller, Dan Morgenstern, Albert Murray, Thomas Owens, Lewis Porter, Doug Richards, Russell Sanjek, Don Schlitten, George T. Simon, Vladimir Simosko, Larry Stempel, Paul Tanner, Hollie I. West, and Rick Woodward.

The following publishers have generously given permission to use extended quotations from copyrighted works: Articles from *Evergreen Review* reprinted by permission of Grove Press. *Four Lives in the Bebop Business* by A.B. Spellman, © 1966 by A.B. Spellman. Reprinted by permission of Pantheon Books, Inc., a division of Random House, Inc. Excerpts from *Jazz Heritage* reprinted by permission of *Saturday Review* magazine © 1964, 1966. *Jazz: Its Evolution and Essence* by André Hodeir, © 1956 by Grove Press. Reprinted by permission. *Jazz Masters of the Twenties* by Richard Hadlock, © 1965 by Richard Hadlock. Reprinted by permission. *Jazz Panorama* edited by Martin Williams, © 1964 by *The Jazz Review,* Inc. Reprinted by permission. *Toward Jazz* by André Hodeir, © 1962 by Grove Press. Reprinted by permission.

Thanks also for permission to excerpt from the works of Aram Avakian, Bourne Co., Fantasy Records, Dick Katz, E.H. Morris and Co., The New York Times Co., RCA Records, Teresa Gramophone Co., Warner Brothers Music, and Warner Special Products.

Contents

66After emancipation . . . all those people . . .
needed the music more than ever . . . trying to find out
from the music what they were supposed to do. . . .
They learned it wasn't just white people the music had to reach to,
nor even their own people, but straight out to life . . .99
—Sidney Bechet

66You've got to love to be able to play.99
—Louis Armstrong

66Music is your own thoughts, your experience, your wisdom.
If you don't live it, it won't come out in your horn.
They teach you there's a boundary line to music.
But, man, there's no boundary line to art.99
—Charlie Parker

66Jazz and freedom go hand in hand.
That explains it. There isn't any more to add to it.
If I do add to it, it gets complicated.
That's something for you to think about.
You think about it and dig it. You dig it.99
—Thelonious Monk

Introduction

Early writers on jazz in the United States frequently pointed out that, as an improvisational music, jazz was well-served by the phonograph, a device that could not only distribute widely what was played in one location but could also preserve for posterity what was made up on the spur of the moment.

The phonograph has accomplished two other things as well: it has shown posterity that in the best jazz, the spontaneity of the moment displays a musicality that endures, and it has allowed musicians all over the world to hear, absorb, and perhaps build on the work of an innovative musician, almost from the moment of his arrival.

The Smithsonian Collection of Classic Jazz is intended as an introduction and an interpretation of seven decades of recorded jazz, as a statement about its major figures, their accomplishments, and their effect. It is also a beginning library of jazz. Necessarily, many worthy figures and groups are left out of it, and others are perhaps not ideally represented. (Does a rare talent like Ben Webster's deserve more than his solos here with Moten and Ellington? Does the absence of John Coltrane's *Giant Steps* unduly neglect an important aspect of his career?)

I hope the set offers a balanced view—balanced in the sense that major figures are given major attention, and balanced under the conviction that once the contributions of such figures are appreciated, the work of their worthy, sometimes distinctive followers will also be clear. For example, if one understands the impact of Louis Armstrong's work, the poised, inventive, straight-ahead solos of a man like Buck Clayton will fall beautifully into place.

The final choices for the contents of this album and its notes are my own. Ultimately they reflect my knowledge of the music's development, my view of its history, and my taste, along with my acquaintance with what others have said and written about the music—necessarily so. But listener-readers are reminded that a major purpose of such a recorded introduction is to encourage them to arrive at their own knowledge and taste and to pursue it wherever it leads them.

The set also serves to remind listeners that final credit goes to the men and women who made this music and to those sometimes anonymous, sometimes visionary, and, yes, sometimes opportunistic people who recorded it for the rest of us.

Duke Ellington once remarked that the pull of American culture is so strong that the rest of the world finds it irresistible, and as a major contributor to our culture, Ellington perhaps knew that to be true better than any of us.

These recordings attest that the pull of the musical culture called jazz is not a matter of the fads and fashions of the moment. It has an honorable, complex, and very human history, and an aesthetic durability in which we can all take pride and, in our ways, participate.

Jazz Music
A Brief History

Trying to Define *Jazz*

Jazz music has been called an American art, America's contribution to the arts, and even an explosion of genius. Jazz has also received a share of praise from those whose main concern has been the traditions of Western European concert music. Composer and critic Virgil Thomson has described it as "the most astounding spontaneous musical event to take place anywhere since the Reformation." One of the earliest published recognitions given to jazz and its importance came in an essay on the clarinetist Sidney Bechet, written in 1919 by the eminent Swiss conductor Ernest Ansermet. Ansermet concluded with the comment that perhaps Bechet's way "is the highway along which the whole world will move tomorrow." The statement was remarkably prophetic, for jazz can now claim devoted listeners and players in every part of the world and every culture where it has been heard. Indeed, jazz may be said to be a universal music, the first the world has known.

Jazz is a major contribution of American black men to contemporary culture. It was they who created it and they who have provided its greatest innovations. At the same time, it has always been a meeting ground: white men have participated since its beginnings, and some of them have contributed with excellence.

Jazz functions as popular art and has enjoyed periods of fairly widespread public response—in the "jazz age" of the 1920s, in the "swing era" of the late 1930s, and in the peak popularity of "modern jazz" in the late 1950s. But as with other artistic pursuits, its most famous and popular figures have not always been its artistic leaders or most important contributors. In 1940 the most popular band was Glenn Miller's, but the artistic honors of that year would go to Duke Ellington, who, as one critic has observed, seemed to produce a masterpiece recording almost every week.

In a preliminary description, jazz might be called an Afro-American musical idiom. Yet we haven't pushed the definition along very far by saying that, because there are many Afro-American musical idioms: field hollers, spirituals, cakewalks, ragtime, blues, black gospel, rhythm-and-blues, rock 'n' roll, to cite only some of them. These idioms are closely related and have

7

often been closely allied with jazz. They have helped form jazz or have influenced it, but one cannot usefully call them jazz.

Jazz and many of its related styles have also been affected by almost all musical idioms to which its players and composers have been exposed: folk and popular musics, "light classics" and even some not-so-light classics. Such influences have also gone in the other direction. American music of all kinds and, indeed, many of the world's musics have felt Afro-American influences at least since the 1860s. By the 1920s, such influences were quite evident in Broadway show tunes, in the concert hall, even in the hillbilly and country-western idioms of the South and the Southwest, and such influences have continued. Jazz has also made major contributions to instrumental concept. For example, hardly anyone today, anywhere in the world, writes for the trumpet without being influenced by what jazz musicians have shown can be done with that instrument.

It is not surprising, then, that beginning in the 1920s and continuing well into the thirties, it was common to apply the word *jazz* rather indiscriminately to almost any music that had been influenced by jazz rhythmically, melodically, or tonally. Thus, George Gershwin was called a jazz composer, and for his concert works he was acclaimed as having made an "honest woman" out of jazz. Somewhat similarly, Paul Whiteman, playing a jazz-influenced dance music, was billed as the King of Jazz. Whiteman's ensemble did provide a haven for some good white jazz musicians, particularly the gifted cornetist Bix Beiderbecke. As for Gershwin, he well knew that jazz was an honest woman to begin with.

Such ensembles as Whiteman's have always been a part of the picture in American music, and some of them have produced good music. In the 1920s, Whiteman, besides occasionally featuring Beiderbecke and other jazzmen, played some scores by arranger Bill Challis that are exceptional in their skill and style. The Stan Kenton orchestra held a comparable position beginning in the late 1940s. Its music, called progressive jazz, offered ambitious orchestrations that were often heavily influenced by the work of early twentieth-century European concert composers. But many musicians and others concerned with the mainstream of jazz development were more apt to praise the later Kenton ensemble (usually called the Young Blood band) which featured such jazz soloists as saxophonists John "Zoot" Sims and Lee Konitz and arrangements by Gerry Mulligan.

In the past, many jazz ensembles, directly and authentically in the mainstream, have in part depended for their popularity on somewhat peripheral features. The Andy Kirk orchestra in the 1930s featured a romantic crooner named Pha Terrell who was quite popular. Similarly, the orchestra of trombonist Tommy Dorsey was as much sustained by its leader's melodious but straightforward interpretation of popular romantic ballads of the time and by the popularity of its singers (Frank Sinatra was one of them) as by the individual and collective abilities of its musicians as jazz players—and perhaps more so.

On the other hand, it might have surprised the avid fans of Kirk, Dorsey, or any of the other swing bands to learn how jazz-influenced were the "sweet" bands of, say Guy Lombardo and Sammy Kaye.

In any case, it does not seem very useful to use the term *jazz* as loosely and casually as has been done, particularly in view of the way the music has succeeded in retaining its identity and has developed since its beginnings.

The origin of the word is itself obscure. However, there is no question but that it was used as a vulgar term for the sex act when it was first applied to the music about 1915. It was initially the white man's name for the music, and thereby revealing of the white man's early response to it.

But one should not give that historical event—that naming of the music—a purely negative interpretation. Jazz has to do with the fundamental rhythms of human life; it has also to do with Western man's contemporary reassessment of his traditional values and of his own nature; and surely, in view of its origins in black American life, jazz has to do with human survival itself. Perhaps, therefore, jazz was not so badly named. At any rate, the name has stuck.

To come somewhat closer to a useful definition, we can say that jazz is primarily a player's art, even when the player works under the guidance of a jazz composer, and that it involves improvisation. Sometimes what is improvised, what is made up by the player himself in performance, is a matter of spontaneous melodic embellishment or the ornamentation of a theme. Sometimes also—for a pianist, say—embellishment may largely involve the harmony, the chords, of a piece, in which these may be variously voiced or substitutions made or passing chords introduced. Sometimes the improvising involves the invention of *new* melody (harmonic variation, in the classical musician's parlance) built only on the harmonic progression or outline (the chord changes, in jazz parlance) of a theme.

One cannot set up an absolute rule about spontaneity, however; some jazz performances may be purely interpretive, but the possibility of spontaneous departure is always there. Jazz is produced in an atmosphere of improvisation, and the ability to extemporize is a part of the jazz soloist's equipment.

Jazz has been played by solo pianists; by pianists in duo with cornet, with clarinet, with string bass; by piano with the accompaniment of string bass and drums; by quasi–brass bands of from five to eight pieces; by quartets and quintets of horns plus rhythm; by "big bands" of twelve to eighteen pieces.

In eighteenth-century Europe, when improvisation was commonly a feature of musical performance, one player or singer—or in the Baroque concerto a small number of featured players—would improvise. In jazz, with certain things usually agreed upon (a tune—or at least its underlying harmonic structure—the relative roles of the instruments, a tempo, a key) as many as eight players might all improvise at once. This happened in the earliest jazz style, in the New Orleans, or dixieland, ensemble.

In recent centuries, Western man has come to make a distinction between popular art and fine art. These distinctions do not always hold up very well (Shakespeare and Dickens were preeminently popular artists), but if we employ them here, jazz (like the movies and the comics) is popular art.

Jazz functions in a milieu where it competes for its audiences with popular musics of various kinds. But jazz is a musical art that has received the highest and most widespread praise and respect and has been awarded much critical and scholarly attention. Further, changes in other popular musics sometimes seem to be matters of caprice or fashion. Jazz, on the other hand, has evolved and developed; its players have learned from and built on the music's past, somewhat in the manner we associate with an art music. And, as jazz historian Stanley Dance has observed, the best musicians have always been ahead of their audiences.

The Blues

Of all the Afro-American idioms in the background of jazz, by far the most important and influential is the blues. Like the word *jazz* itself, the word *blues* presents difficulties because it has been subject to careless usage and misunderstanding. As used in jazz, *blues* does not describe a melancholy or sad mood; it refers to a definite musical form which has been used to express a variety of moods. That form does not seem to have originated either in Africa or in Europe, but represents a coming-together of elements from both traditions, a coming-together brought about largely by Afro-Americans and probably dating back to pre-Emancipation times.

Like much music, the blues undoubtedly began as a kind of slow, rhythmic chant or lament. At least by the teens of this century, however, its music and its words had come to have a regular and apparently generally accepted form.

Musically, *blues* had come to mean a regular twelve-measure form, usually harmonized (in one of its simpler versions) with four measures on a I chord, two on a IV chord, two back to a I, two on a V, then a final two back to I. In B-flat, this would be four bars on a B-flat chord, two on an E-flat, two on a B-flat, two on an F, and two on a B-flat.

To the layman, however, the blues form is best known through its vocal version and its verse, or stanza, form: a line (of approximate iambic pentameter length), the same line repeated exactly (or almost exactly), plus a third line with a terminal rhyme:

> *Don't the moon look lonesome shinin' through the trees.*
> *Yes, the moon looks lonesome, shinin' through the trees.*
> *Don't your house look lonesome when your baby packs up to leave.*

Some quite simple blues achieve a high degree of poetry in their lyrics. More important from a musical standpoint, however, the blues was sung with melodic spontaneity (if the singer could manage it) and with high emotion manifest in various bent, quavered, and freely inflected pitches and tones. These resources are common in African music and are analogous to practices in others of the world's musics as well.

When the blues came to be written down in Western notation—around the teens of this century—and played on Western instruments, the standard was to the European system of pitch and, more specifically, the tuning of the piano keyboard. It became conventional to represent the bent tones of the blues by lowering, or flatting, the third and seventh (later also the fifth) step of the scale, and these came to be called the blue notes. Thus, a sort of minor scale resulted:

● = a blue note, which may be as much as a half tone above or below the written pitch.

In practice, the bent notes come almost anywhere the singer or player wants or feels them, but instrumentalists most often tend to flat the third, seventh, and sometimes fifth.

For a singer, bending a note is simple enough, and the player of a stringed instrument can readily finger bent tones. Other instrumentalists "lip" these notes, and brass players can also use "half valve" effects and a variety of mutes. Even jazz pianists have learned to produce a "curved" or "bent" sound, through a particular manipulation of touch, finger position, and pedal. Thelonious Monk was expert at such tonal and textural manipulations.

The blues had become an instrumental as well as a vocal form at least by the early 1920s, and probably earlier. A player or group of players could improvise blues melodies (or interpret indigenous or traditional ones) for as many choruses as inspiration held up, using as a guide the twelve-measure form and blues harmonic outline, repeated in cycles.

Trumpeter Henry "Red" Allen once said of playing the blues: "It's like somebody making your lip speak, making it say things he thinks....The blues is a slow story. The feeling of the beautiful things that happen to you is in the blues; it's a home language, like two friends talking. It's the language everybody understands."

One significant fact is that as the instrumental blues were refined and developed, the blue notes did not get refined away or "corrected" but were retained right along with other aspects of the music. Furthermore, players were expected to find their own sounds, their own voices, on their instruments just the way the singers did. And blues practices came to be applied to other forms. Thus, in 1947 a "modern" jazzman improvising on a theme like Jerome Kern's *All the Things You Are* could use a personal melodic invention and employ the blues scale in this quite different context.

As suggested above, some melodies with *blues* in their titles are not really blues. This applies not only to popular songs like *Singin' the Blues* and *I Gotta Right to Sing the Blues* but occasionally to the jazz repertory as well: Jelly Roll Morton's *Wolverine Blues* is not in a twelve-measure form, and neither is Duke Ellington's masterful *Old Man Blues*.

There are other kinds of blues besides the twelve-measure kind. *How Long, How Long* and *Trouble in Mind* are familiar examples of eight-bar (eight-measure) blues, which more or less condense the twelve-bar kind. And there are sixteen-measure blues which more or less expand it (Louis Armstrong's *Potato Head Blues* in this album, for example). Then there is another sixteen-measure structure borrowed from the European tradition of such songs as *Old MacDonald Had a Farm,* which jazz musicians have treated as blues. Examples would range from Jimmy Noone's *My Daddy Rocks Me,* recorded in the 1920s, through Sonny Rollins's *Doxy,* from the late 1950s. There is also a "refrain" variant of the twelve-measure blues, well-known examples of which include *Why Don't You Do Right?* and *Blue Suede Shoes.*

By the 1920s, the vocal blues tradition had produced a great artist in singer Bessie Smith, whose works include simple twelve-measure pieces like *Lost Your Head Blues* and rather ingeniously combined forms such as those in *Young Woman's Blues.* Furthermore, there is often a delicate artistic balance maintained between the power of Smith's singing, the poetry of her verses, and the interplaying comments of her accompanists.

The vocal blues tradition has remained a vital one. In the 1950s the music had come to be called rhythm and blues and in this manifestation became a progenitor of rock 'n' roll. Similarly, boogie woogie, which found national popularity in the late 1930s (but is actually much older), is a percussive blues piano style.

The first publicly successful blues man was W. C. Handy. Handy could be called a kind of inspired folklorist, who took indigenous melodies he heard around him, polished them, and built them into blues song structures, which could also serve as instrumental compositions.

Handy's *St. Louis Blues* (1914) contains three separate sections, each with its own melody and all very well balanced, one with the next. In building his pieces this way, Handy was modeling them on the compositions in the Afro-American style that had meanwhile appeared around the turn of the century, the style called ragtime. If the blues may be said to have given jazz its soul, then ragtime gave it important and durable early structure and form.

Scott Joplin in one of the few surviving photographs, 1904.

Ragtime

Piano ragtime began to be published in the late 1890s. It was immediately successful and almost immediately subjected to various kinds of popularization, almost all of which have continued. It was (and is) sometimes played fast and shallow, with deliberately stiff rhythms, on a jangling "prepared" piano—so much so that it is difficult to convince some listeners that the early ragtime composers were highly gifted melodists and serious craftsmen who produced an admirable body of musical art.

Ragtime was basically a piano keyboard music and, one might say, an Afro-American version of the polka, or its analog, the Sousa-style march. Thus, the first great rag composition, *Maple Leaf Rag,* by the first great rag composer, Scott Joplin, is built on four melodies, or themes. If we assign a letter to each theme, the structure of *Maple Leaf* comes out to ABACD. In rags, these themes were of sixteen measures (or sometimes eight and rarely thirty-two measures), like their European counterparts.

There is every reason to believe that a rich body of Afro-American-inspired music preceded ragtime, although there are no recordings from those years. Certainly the cakewalk, an Afro-American dance initially based on an elegant, stylized parody of Southern white courtly manners, preceded it, and there was published cakewalk music, although publishers in those days were not quite sure how to indicate its rhythms properly.

But ragtime introduced, in the accents of its right-hand melodies, delightful syncopations onto the heavy 2/4 *oompah* rhythm of its cakewalk-derived bass line and almost immediately became a kind of national, even worldwide craze. Besides Joplin, who was a prolific composer during his short life, it offered such gifted writers as James Scott, Tom Turpin, and a white contributor, Joseph Lamb.

New Orleans

Anyone acquainted with the early jazz repertory will notice that in such dixieland standards as, let us say, *Jazz Me Blues* or *Muskrat Ramble* is reflected the same multi-themed structure as in ragtime. But there are important differences. Early jazz was usually played by a small "band" of from five to eight pieces, with a definite instrumental style. There is more variety in jazz rhythms, and there seems to be greater emotional range and depth (an infusion of the feeling of the blues is the answer here).

The music that came to be called jazz first developed in New Orleans. Initially it appears to have evolved somewhat parallel to ragtime, beginning about 1900, and when it encountered the great rags, it absorbed and transformed them. The first group to popularize the New Orleans idiom outside its home city and record it was a white ensemble called the Original Dixieland Jazz Band. Opinions on the musical merit and importance of that group differ today, but it created a popular sensation in New York in 1917, and it acquainted a wide international public with its version of the New Orleans idiom.

New Orleans jazz is played in a kind of polyphony, in which a trumpet (or trumpets)—cornet in the early days—states a melody, with such embellishments and departures as the trumpeter may feel during a performance. Simultaneously, a clarinet improvises a counter-melody above and around the trumpet; a trombone improvises a simpler melody, a kind of ground bass, below the trumpet; and a rhythm section, consisting of drums, a plucked string bass (occasionally a tuba), a guitar (occasionally a banjo), and piano, provide an interplaying harmonic-rhythmic accompaniment. (The rhythm section in smaller groups may be smaller, merely piano and drums, say; or the piano may be omitted but the three others retained, etc.) There are ad lib solos, but in the very early days these were apparently only exchanges of the lead instrument (clarinet over a subdued trumpet for a chorus, say) or simply bolder embellishments by the trumpeter.

New Orleans jazz produced many great and influential figures, cornetists Freddie Keppard and Joseph "King" Oliver, clarinetist and soprano saxophonist Sidney Bechet, clarinetists Jimmy Noone and Johnny Dodds among them. But perhaps the best overall view of its achievements can be seen through the work of two figures, composer-pianist Ferdinand "Jelly

Jelly Roll Morton and His Red Hot Peppers: from left, Andrew Hilaire, Kid Ory, George Mitchell, Johnny Lindsay, Morton, Johnny St. Cyr, Omer Simeon. (Duncan Schiedt Collection)

Roll" Morton and trumpeter Louis Armstrong. Morton's work brilliantly synthesized what the idiom had accomplished; Armstrong's grandiloquence showed the music and its players what to do next.

Ferdinand "Jelly Roll" Morton

Jelly Roll Morton faced and solved the problem of the role of a pianist, composer, and ensemble leader in an improvisational music. Morton's best recordings balance the individual and the group, the soloist and the ensemble, in performances that are continuous wholes greater than the sum of their individual parts.

His great ensemble works were recorded somewhat late in the development of the style, beginning in 1926. Pieces like *Dead Man Blues, Black Bottom Stomp,* and *Grandpa's Spells* use several themes, polyphony, harmonized passages, soloists, and various smaller and unusual instrumental combinations, with a continuity and a developing order and balance.

Aside from its intrinsic merit, Morton's music also reflects the changes that had taken place in the New Orleans style, which are perhaps best understood as rhythmic changes. To go back for a moment, most cakewalk music is notated in 2/4 time with two alternate heavy beats per bar. Ragtime is still a music in 2/4, but, as we have seen, its melodies add anticipatory syncopations. In New Orleans, when the form of ragtime came together with the soul of the blues, more rhythmic variety was introduced, and the basic pulse moved from 2/4 to 4/4 time.

Morton also was adept at using the *habañera* rhythm (his "jazz tangos" like *Mamanita, Creepy Feeling,* and the tango blues *New Orleans Joys*—or *New Orleans Blues*—are fine examples), which in jazz soon became the Charleston rhythm.

Louis Armstrong

Morton's virtues were those of a perceptive composer-orchestrator working in an improvisational idiom. Cornetist, trumpeter, and singer Louis Armstrong was a single improvising soloist and innovator. The older New Orleans players were apt to say that Armstrong achieved fully all the things they had been working on. Other musicians, and eventually the followers and fans of the music as well, were so taken with his innovations and the unique rhythmic variety and momentum in his work that eventually they had to come up with a new word for a new style, *swing.*

Armstrong first attracted attention in Chicago in the early 1920s as a member of the New Orleans-style ensemble of King Oliver. He was an excellent trumpeter, an inventive melodist, and a great blues player, but perhaps his greatest talent lay in his ability to transform even the most banal of popular melodies. To achieve this, he might anticipate one phrase of the original, slightly delay the next, heighten a good turn of melody, and omit a weak or inferior one, substituting one of his own. He could take the most ordinary song and transmute it into a compelling instrumental experience. To describe such Armstrong solos, unique combinations of melodic variation and outright invention of melody, French critic André Hodeir has borrowed the term *paraphrase.*

Among Armstrong's most celebrated recordings are his blues inventions like *S.O.L. Blues* and *Potato Head Blues,* his eloquent paraphrases of popular songs like *I Can't Give You Anything But Love, That's My Home, I Gotta Right to Sing the Blues,* and his collaborations with pianist Earl Hines like *Skip the Gutter, Weather Bird,* and *West End Blues.*

That latter, from 1928, is one of the most advanced and mature Armstrong recordings, and along with *Sweethearts on Parade* (1930), *Between the Devil and the Deep Blue Sea* (take 3, 1931), and his second (1933) version of *Basin Street Blues,* it goes beyond even the era that he founded and reaches well into the style of the middle 1940s.

Swing Bands

In 1924 Armstrong was in New York, a member of the Fletcher Henderson orchestra, whose chief composer and arranger was Don Redman. From that triple collaboration came the foundations of big band jazz, which eventually found wide public popularity in the middle 1930s and began the "swing era."

By 1932 Henderson was composing and arranging for his orchestra himself, using an ensemble of three trumpets, two trombones, three or four saxophones (doubling on clarinets), and four rhythm instruments. The arrangements pitted one section against the other in a kind of call-and-response, antiphonal style (the saxophones might sing out the opening phrase of a piece, and the trumpets then respond with an instrumental "Yes, indeed!"). Then there were the riffs (brief, repeated, strongly rhythmic phrases of one or two bars). Also featured were *written* variations, for section or sections, and, of course, improvised solos.

It was this style that Henderson later passed on as Benny Goodman's staff arranger, and it was Goodman who played it to great success. Such Goodman recordings as *Down South Camp Meeting, Wrappin' It Up,* and *Big John Special* were first recorded by Henderson's own ensemble.

Duke Ellington

Almost all the successful big bands of the time used a style derived from Henderson's. The outstanding exception was the ensemble of pianist-composer Edward Kennedy "Duke" Ellington.

Ellington, working closely with his players, became the jazz composer–orchestra leader *par excellence.* He perfected the big band style, he used the American dance band as a vehicle for personal artistic expression, and he has been called America's greatest composer.

Ellington's music retained the spontaneity and earthy eloquence of the basic idiom in sometimes highly sophisticated treatments and settings. Redman and Henderson used the sections of the jazz orchestra in a compartmentalized way, as we have seen: the saxes did this, the trumpets did that, and the trombones did the other, if they did not join with the trumpets. A saxophone or clarinet soloist regularly got a brass accompaniment, a trumpet soloist was accompanied by the saxes, and so on. Ellington explored the sonorous possibilities and resources of the jazz orchestra in combinations of sounds and notes and instruments, muted and unmuted, along with the individual talents of his players in both solo and ensemble combinations.

He undertook every kind of music from long concert works, like *Reminiscing in Tempo, Suite Thursday,* and *Black, Brown and Beige,* to brief successful popular songs like *I'm Beginning to See the Light* and *Don't Get Around Much Anymore.* And there are excellences from every period of his career from the mid-1920s onward.

But we are apt to think of the great Ellington period as from 1938 to 1942 and to think of the great Ellington works as not his songs but his instrumental pieces such as *Blue Light, Subtle Lament, Ko-Ko, Rumpus in Richmond, Harlem Air Shaft, Concerto for Cootie, Sepia Panorama,* and *Blue Serge.*

All of these works are collaborations between Ellington and his sidemen and soloists—chiefly, at this period, trumpeter Charles "Cootie" Williams, cornetist Rex Stewart, trombonists Lawrence Brown, Juan Tizol, and Joe Nanton, clarinetist Barney Bigard, tenor saxophonist Ben Webster, alto saxophonist Johnny Hodges, and baritone saxophonist Harry Carney.

In such performances, Ellington rediscovered in far more sophisticated terms what Morton had found in his own idiom: the perfect balance between what is written ahead of time and what can be ad-libbed in performance, what is up to the individual and what the ensemble contributes, what makes an effective part and what makes a continuous, encompassing, subsuming whole.

Ellington was born in Washington, D.C., and gained youthful experience as both a player and bandleader there. Among his early influences were the Harlem post-ragtime "stride" pianists (so-called because of the rhythmic quality of their playing, an extension of the oompah ragtime left hand), men like James P. Johnson and his unofficial pupil Thomas "Fats" Waller. But Ellington was apparently not sure of his own style, or of his destiny, until the emotionally charged improvising of his own players inspired him to become a jazz composer. Outstanding among his early associates was the trumpeter James "Bubber" Miley, a more than able man with mutes, who contributed both as composer and player to such important early Ellingtonia as *East St. Louis Toddle-o, The Mooche,* and *Black and Tan Fantasy.*

Fletcher Henderson had made a jazz band out of a conventional American dance band of the period. Ellington's beginnings as a truly individual orchestrator date from a 1927-31 engagement at the Cotton Club in New York when his orchestra became a "show band," or "pit band," playing for the skits, chorus routines, and specialty dances of a night club show as well as providing music when the club's patrons had their turn on the floor. It was while working in such a dual capacity that he began to discover the orchestral textures and colors and resources that characterize his best work.

Ellington's recordings, like all good jazz, repay the closest kind of listening.

What is Swing?

Louis Armstrong inspired musicians of all kinds all over the world. Within jazz, he inspired composers and arrangers, ensembles both large and small, and individual soloists on all instruments. But that is not to say that the outstanding instrumentalists and singers of the time were merely imitating him.

Tenor saxophonist Coleman Hawkins, for example, can be heard on Fletcher Henderson's *Stampede* or his 1928 version of *King Porter Stomp* in solos that depend on Armstrong's early trumpet style, but by the 1933 Henderson version of *New King Porter Stomp*, the influence clearly has been assimilated. In this and his later solos, such as the celebrated *Body and Soul,* Hawkins had a personal style based on an adroit use of arpeggios and a melodic rhythm more regular in its accent pattern than Armstrong's.

Similarly, trumpeter Roy Eldridge paid homage to Armstrong, but in such solos as his *Rockin' Chair, I Surrender Dear,* and *After You've Gone,* he used Armstrong's ideas in a spare and almost indirect way.

So did pianist Teddy Wilson, vibraharpist Lionel Hampton, trombonists Jack Teagarden and Dickie Wells, and the dozens of other outstanding improvisors of the era. Billie Holiday, the great singer of the time, had a talent for the melodic paraphrase of popular ditties that was almost as sublime as Armstrong's, and a dramatic power of unique strength.

Pianist Art Tatum learned the rhythmic lessons of swing, but he was a player with a superb harmonic imagination and outstanding keyboard technique. His approach to melody, however, was usually through embellishment and ornamentation rather than paraphrase or outright invention.

One might say that jazz musicians spent the late twenties and early thirties absorbing Armstrong's rhythmic ideas, the basis of his swing. Some of the soloists grasped them quite early; it took a bit longer for the ensembles to achieve a *collective* swing, though the best of them had it in hand by 1932.

That term *swing* is obviously more than a catchword or even the name of a period in jazz history. It has become a part of the technical vocabulary of jazz and has to do with using the rhythmic shadings and nuances that are appropriate to the music. *Swing* has never been properly defined (although more than one critic has tried the job), but it is empirically present (or not present) in a performance, and it imparts a special quality of momentum.

As we have seen, the term came in with Louis Armstrong and was applied to a style in which his influence was strongly felt. It has been retained in discussing subsequent styles, and it has even been applied retroactively to earlier styles. That is, *swing* has been used to mean the rhythmic quality proper to an early New Orleans ensemble performance and even to a ragtime piano solo.

Count Basie, Lester Young, and Charlie Christian

By the mid-thirties there appeared a big band that was beginning to go a bit beyond swing in the 1932 sense. It was the innovative orchestra of pianist William "Count" Basie, which came out of Kansas City in 1936.

At that period the Basie band's style was actually a simplification of Fletcher Henderson's style, but with a special ensemble spirit as well as a greater emphasis on the soloist. The rhythm section played with a new lightness, and the rhythmic lead was taken not by Jo Jones's light, foot-cymbal-oriented drums but by Walter Page's strong string bass. The leader's piano was basically a simplification of previous styles (his early influences had been Fats Waller and Earl Hines), but he played it with a light yet percussive touch that has defied imitation, and an often witty sense of order.

The greatest of the Basie soloists was tenor saxophonist Lester Young, who played lighter and more legato than the Hawkins-influenced saxophonists and with a sprightly, imaginative variety in rhythm, accent, and phrase.

Count Basie in 1939. *(Duncan Schiedt Collection)*

Basie's most famous performance is the instrumental blues *One O'Clock Jump;* classic early Basie recordings include *Doggin' Around, Time Out, Taxi War Dance,* and the small ensemble masterpiece *Lester Leaps In.*

There was one player who absorbed and built upon Lester Young's innovations early: guitarist Charlie Christian, who had a brief, brilliant public career as a member of the Benny Goodman Sextet between late 1939 and his death in early 1942. Almost any of Christian's recorded solos is exceptional (*I Found a New Baby* and *Profoundly Blue* are classic improvisations), and he is also one of the few jazz musicians of the time whose work in jam sessions got recorded and has been released on commercial recordings.

Modern Jazz and Charlie Parker

The middle 1940s were a period in which the ideas of Lester Young and Charlie Christian (and the most advanced work of Armstrong as well) were built upon and elaborated into a style that involved major innovation. The participants were many—drummers Kenny Clarke and Max Roach, pianists Thelonious Monk and Earl "Bud" Powell, bassist Oscar Pettiford, and others— and the emphasis switched from big bands to small groups, usually quintets. Chiefly this new music centered around the work of trumpeter John "Dizzy" Gillespie and alto saxophonist Charlie Parker. Once again, the harmonic and melodic innovations in the music centered around rhythmic innovations, and so, once again, there had to be a new onomatopoeic catch-name for the style: *bebop.*

Parker was a brilliant, inventive melodist whose spontaneous imagination seemed, within the confines of his style, virtually inexhaustible. Harmonically he was as imaginative as Art Tatum or, to pick a saxophonist, Coleman Hawkins's exceptional follower, Don Byas. Rhythmically, Parker went beyond even Young and Christian. His accents might fall on strong beats (1 and 3 in a measure in 4/4 time) or weak beats (2 and 4), or in a subtle variety of places in between beats. Yet for all the overflowing variety of his playing, his best solos have a rare sense of order. Often this was based on a constructive contrast of brief, rhythmically terse phrases alternating with long, flowing bursts of lyric melody, or sometimes on a sequential use and development of brief recurring motives in more complex and subtle ways than his predecessors.

It has been said that such improvisations as Parker's *Embraceable You,* which make no melodic reference to the written songs but only use their chord sequences, came in with the jazz of the 1940s. But that is obviously untrue. Indeed, there are examples of such harmonic variations in jazz that go back to the players of the 1920s, as the music in this album will show. Similarly, the business of *writing* new and more jazzlike themes to the chord sequences of established songs goes back quite far. An example in this set is the 1932 *Moten Swing* of the Benny Moten band, which borrows its harmonic structure from *You're Driving Me Crazy.*

The most commonly used chord structure in jazz after the blues is that borrowed from George Gershwin's *I Got Rhythm*. It is the opening section of Sidney Bechet's *Shag* (1932), and it provides the basis for hundreds of pieces and improvised solos throughout the thirties, forties, and fifties by small ensembles and big bands. The celebrated Woody Herman Orchestra of the mid-1940s, known as the Herman Herd among its fans, was called the *I Got Rhythm* band among musicians because so much of its repertory was based on that piece's chord sequence.

In the late forties there also arrived a group of players who were initially more influenced by Lester Young than Charlie Parker. They included pianist Lennie Tristano; his early associate, alto saxophonist Lee Konitz; tenor saxophonist Stan Getz; and baritone saxophonist and composer Gerry Mulligan.

In the jazz of the forties and fifties, the harmonic language became increasingly chromatic, even impressionistic, and players undertook sophisticated popular melodies such as *All the Things You Are, How High the Moon,* and *I'll Remember April.* At the same time, they continued to embrace the traditional challenge of the blues; indeed, the flatted-fifth blue note became firmly established through their use of it. And the music kept, and expanded, its basic rhythmic vitality.

Thelonious Monk and Form for Modern Jazz

In a good performance by Louis Armstrong or by Charlie Parker, the trumpeter or the saxophonist is apt to be so brilliant that he becomes the whole show. No matter how good the accompaniment or the other soloists' improvisations, the main part is the leader's. But in a successful Morton or Ellington recording, the point is the quality of the whole, no matter how well any individual player may acquit himself.

From what has preceded, it may seem that major and influential events in jazz history center around its composers, who give the music synthesis and overall form, and around individual innovative soloists, who periodically renew its musical vocabulary. And further, these events seem to alternate; that is, from Morton's synthesis to Armstrong's innovations to Ellington's synthesis to Parker's innovations.

If that is so, then one might expect a major composer-leader to emerge after Parker, but it turned out that that composer had been around for some time. After Parker's early death in 1955, musicians began to turn for guidance to the work of pianist-composer Thelonious Monk. Monk had been an exceptional composer and small-ensemble leader all along; some of his best recordings had been made between 1948 and 1954.

Monk's sense of form was less studied than Ellington's, and in the little quartets, quintets, and sextets with which he most often worked, form itself was improvisational: a performance might discover its own form almost as it

Thelonious Monk, the unique. *(Photo by Charles Stewart)*

developed. Monk was also an apparently (but deceptively) simple pianist, who sacrificed much conventional technique in order to develop techniques of his own.

Two of Monk's associates on some of his classic recordings were vibraphonist Milt Jackson and tenor saxophonist Theodore "Sonny" Rollins, and the further work of each of these men offered additional evidence that the jazz of the 1950s was discovering and searching out ensemble style and form that might also use the innovations of Parker, Gillespie, and Monk. Jackson became a member of the superb Modern Jazz Quartet which, under the musical direction of its pianist, John Lewis, contributed outstanding performances, such as *Django,* a piece the group recorded several times, and always well.

Rollins became virtually a one-man ensemble, contributing, for two examples, an architectonic set of variations on *Blue 7* and a kind of improvisational jazz rondo on *Blues for Philly Joe* (named for drummer Joe Jones from Philadelphia).

Meanwhile, a composer and bassist of importance had emerged in Charles Mingus. An outstanding soloist, in ensemble playing Mingus not only carried the basic 4/4 pulse of a performance, he provided a bass line of such interest and variety that it ceased to be an accompaniment in the old sense and became a contrapuntal part, participating far more directly in the spontaneous musical texture.

Jazz Rhythm and Jazz History

One can tell much of the story of jazz by recounting the developments within the rhythm section and the responses of its players to the innovations introduced by the horn men. In the light of subsequent jazz history, one can say that the New Orleans section had a kind of built-in redundancy of function, with all players (one way or another) counting off the basic 1-2-3-4 of the pulse. Count Basie showed that the pianist's left hand need not keep this basic time, and in the Basie ensemble, bassist Walter Page took the rhythmic lead away from the drummer. Soon thereafter, rhythm guitar, playing chords four-to-a-bar, virtually disappeared from the big band.

In the bebop, or modern jazz, rhythm section of the mid-1940s, there were further refinements. The drummer might confine his time-keeping to one ride cymbal, while using all else—even the foot pedal of the bass drums on occasion—to improvise a percussive line that interplayed polyrhythmically with the basic pulse and with the melodic rhythm of the soloists. In some "free jazz" and "new thing" rhythm sections of the 1960s and seventies, the basic pulse might be understood or felt by all concerned but regularly stated by no one.

As we have seen, traditionally most jazz has been in 4/4 time, but other meters have been used on occasion: 3/4 waltzes go back to ragtime, and 6/8 waltzes became fairly common by the late 1950s. There have been experiments, particularly in the late fifties by the popular Dave Brubeck Quartet, Horace Silver's Quintet, and others, with unusual time signatures. It would seem, however, that both the polyrhythmic texture of earlier jazz and the free and varied rhythms employed by the "new thing" musicians provide ultimate responses to such efforts.

"Free Jazz"—the "New Thing"

Two major events in the new jazz of the 1960s took place at virtually the same moment but apparently with no cross-influence. In New York trumpeter Miles Davis, who had been an early associate of Charlie Parker and had gone on to be an important musician himself, led a recital called, on its LP release, *Kind of Blue*. In effect, Davis asked himself and his men to take a different and perhaps more risky approach to improvisation, not only to discard melodic embellishment and paraphrase but also to forego a chord progression and a harmonic outline as guides for inventing jazz solos.

Thus, on *So What,* in the *Kind of Blue* album, regular eight-bar phrases of the AABA piece are followed, but the players are assigned only the notes of the D-Dorian mode (a white-key piano scale D to D) as melodic and harmonic material, plus, in the bridge, an E-flat Dorian mode, (the same scale a half step up). And in *Flamenco Sketches,* each soloist uses a succession of five scales, employing each for as long as he wishes and then taking up the next.

Virtually simultaneously with the release of *Kind of Blue,* an almost unknown alto saxophonist, Ornette Coleman, released his first important recording, undertook an extended engagement in New York, and received his first national recognition.

Coleman had been working in Los Angeles, on a music in which, similarly, improvisation did not follow a preset sequence of chords, and in which a soloist need not follow the phrases of a theme—that is, a variation on an eight-bar phrase might take six bars. But perhaps the most striking aspect of Coleman's playing was his use of microtones (intervals smaller than a half tone). Whole passages might be obliquely intoned, played deliberately sharp or flat, for emotional or interpretive effect—an extension of the idea of blue notes and other personally inflected sounds of earlier jazz. And in Coleman's quartets and trios, even an opening theme might be freely interpreted by two instrumentalists, though they are stating it together. (There are obvious analogies between the improvising of Coleman's quartets and trios and the practices of Eastern, particularly Indian, music.)

Individually, Coleman's own accents and melodic rhythms may seem quite simple, even old-fashioned, but the variety of accent, phrase, and rhythm he employs within an improvisation offers a new kind of freedom to the jazzman. Similarly, in *The Riddle,* Coleman's group executes collective, spontaneous changes of tempo to follow the soloist's inspiration.

For all his "freedom," Coleman is still an orderly improvisor with an outstanding capacity for developing a few key ideas, or motives, which recur in his extended solos like designs in an elaborate tapestry.

One player who came under Coleman's influence was tenor saxophonist John Coltrane, a participant in the Davis *Kind of Blue* album. One might say that Coltrane spent most of the rest of his career developing some of the implications of that recording, but in the years just before his untimely death in 1967, he began also to be influenced by Coleman. Among Coleman's other outstanding followers were trumpeter Don Cherry, who played on the saxophonist's earliest recordings and composed the very interesting extended work *Complete Communion,* and Albert Ayler, a tenor saxophonist in whose work the influences of both Coltrane and Coleman were discernable.

Gunther Schuller remarked in 1958 that Thelonious Monk's music had pushed jazz through the European harmonic system and brought it "to the brink of atonality." It is characteristic of the music and its determination to keep its own identity that it has found its own way into areas of atonality— that is, music without a fixed key center—rather than borrow atonal practice wholesale (although some jazzmen have subsequently done that also). For although Coleman's melodic lines are frequently modal, they are freely intoned, and sometimes he does move out of key. The ensemble collectively is allowed an atmosphere of atonality in the juxtaposition of the soloist's line and the lines of the string bass, which moves in a kind of melodic and dissonant counterpoint.

The Seventies and Early Eighties: Exploration, Fusion, and Conservatism

There is a truism that recent events are more difficult to view in proper perspective than those of the more distant past, but this should never encourage us to avoid the effort. What follows is a necessarily brief evaluation of some events in jazz in the past decade and a half.

In the 1970s certain observers declared jazz to be dead (as some observers had done previously). But jazz musicians—whether or not they were reaching fewer people than before—went on playing everywhere they could (as jazz musicians always do). They also came up with innovations that proved controversial (as their innovations usually do).

It is perhaps ironic, and it is surely a sign of a musical retrenchment, that early in the decade much attention centered on certain pianists: McCoy Tyner, who had been John Coltrane's pianist; Keith Jarrett—*In Front* is an excellent example of his work—who sometimes used Ornette Coleman's early sidemen; and Chick Corea, whose modal blues *Matrix*, particularly, was widely played. Leadership from pianists is ironic in view of the fact that Coleman's music, and Coltrane's later music, depend so much on the use of microtones, and (unless the instrument is doctored) the piano cannot reproduce such tones.

Corea, along with several other soon-to-be-prominent younger musicians, participated in a two-record set of Miles Davis's called *Bitches Brew,* and with that album the movement called *fusion* gained focus and momentum.

Jazz musicians have always given their attention to whatever music has surrounded them, and they have managed to absorb whatever they wanted— from Sousa marches and the tango through the works of the great Broadway tunesmiths to the Brazilian bossa nova in the 1960s. So it is not surprising that the fusion of jazz and other popular idioms of the 1970s should have been undertaken. But the effort was not entirely new. Soul singer Ray Charles and his band had been offering a kind of jazz-rock for several years. The Thad Jones--Mel Lewis Orchestra had recorded an outstanding boogaloo blues in *Central Park North.* Davis himself had begun his efforts on his LPs *In a Silent Way* and *Sorcerer.* And the Modern Jazz Quartet was soon offering a jazz-reggae in *Walkin' Stomp.*

Bitches Brew (1969), in its various selections, sought to fuse jazz with almost every idiom that was popular at the time, and spinoffs soon followed. Members of the group called Weather Report offered an electronic jazz-rock; pianist Herbie Hancock a jazz--rhythm and blues; Chick Corea a kind of jazz-salsa in his Return to Forever group; and certainly Davis himself, on the jazz-soul *Miles Runs the Voodoo Down* (for one), which achieved an intensity that is rare, even for him.

However, although some observers—including some outstanding musicians—saw fusion, and most particularly jazz-rock, as an honorable effort, others—again including some outstanding musicians—saw it as a kind of commercial opportunism. Trumpeter Clark Terry, a former associate of both Basie and Ellington, raised an essential problem for a jazz-rock music when he observed that jazz rhythm seems to be lean and to move forward, but the beat in rock 'n' roll is heavy and seems to bounce in one spot.

That description certainly fits rock dancing, which involves relatively little horizontal motion by the dancers. Rock and fusion have also virtually abandoned the device musicians call "jazz eighth notes" or "swinging eighth notes," a way of phrasing and accenting that also gives momentum to the music.

The early 1980s saw the arrival of a singular group for jazz and a singular event in jazz history. David Murray, Hamiet Bluiett, Julius Hemphill and Oliver Lake—all saxophonists, doubling on various other reeds and flutes—formed the World Saxophone Quartet. Its arrival can be compared to the advent of the string quartet in European music—that is, a distillation of the previous ensemble to an essential few instruments and a discovery, in that distillation, of a new musical style.

For one thing, the WSQ dealt head-on with a problem that has been there in small-ensemble jazz since the beginning. Although the jazz rhythm section has been through many changes since the tuba replaced the string bass in the 1920s and the guitar dropped out in the 1940s, we nevertheless find the same number of instruments (three) supporting one or two horns as support a sixteen-piece orchestra—an obvious imbalance. The World Saxophone Quartet has dropped the rhythm section altogether and given the music a truly new kind of small ensemble.

Further, some of the group's performances are, like a handful of Thelonious Monk's recordings, so much all-of-a-piece that one might be hard put to decide what is composed, what is arranged ahead of time, and what is improvised in performance.

In the music of the World Saxophone Quartet there is also a coming together of the fruits of two decades of modal and free jazz. Perhaps the group offers, on a small scale, the same kind of comprehensive ensemble synthesis of what had preceded them as Morton, Ellington, and Monk did before them.

Using The Recordings

The listener is, of course, invited to use the collection any way he chooses. He can play the records historically, as they are programmed on the LPs, or selectively, for pleasure, enlightenment, or the most casual kind of listening. But one proposition behind a compilation like this one is that jazz repays careful listening by anyone. So, for the listener who wants to dig in a little more deeply, a few suggestions.

Hearing the Melody

For the uninitiated, one of the most puzzling aspects of jazz is the question of the melody and what happens to it. After all, in great numbers of jazz performances, we are dealing with songs from the popular repertory, songs which, however artfully put together, are often relatively simple and readily singable by most of us. From these songs, jazzmen often fashion their performances.

The first thing to say about a jazzman's use of a melody is that even if he plays it quite straightforwardly, with a minimum of change from the way it was written, he is free to interpret and pronounce it in his own way— indeed he is required to do so. Perhaps the simplest and most direct statement of a familiar popular song melody by a jazz instrumentalist in this album is Benny Goodman's opening reading of *Body and Soul*. And yet his handling of both the theme and the sound of his clarinet are personal. On the other hand, Goodman's opening chorus in *I Found a New Baby* is looser in departing from the original.

There are several musicians in this album whose general approach is to base almost everything they do somehow on the melody itself. Erroll Garner is in this style, a master of such thematic variations. And anyone might follow the familiar melody in an Art Tatum performance, even though the pianist's ornamentations and embellishments and enhancements are dazzlingly intricate.

Thelonious Monk also takes a thematic approach, but his way of embellishing is at times almost opposite to Tatum's. Monk cuts back, distills—

indeed one might say that he is apt to bring out hidden qualities in a piece by leaving out as much as Tatum adds.

Louis Armstrong's spontaneous rewriting of a melody is apt to seem simpler than it actually is. Under scrutiny his eloquent simplification of *I Gotta Right to Sing the Blues* or his elaborate recasting of *Sweethearts on Parade* contain intuitive subtleties in what he uses from the original, what he changes slightly, and what he adds of his own that are evidence of personal melodic genius.

On the other hand, one will find solo after solo in this album with apparently no melodic and thematic connection with the original. These are the kinds of jazz improvisations that sometimes give new listeners the most trouble.

These solos are harmonic variations; that is, they use the harmony of the piece, the chord progression, as a guide, and not the melody. We might say that they use the skeleton or the outline (or the left hand piano part) and make up a new melody to fit it.

Let's go back to *Body and Soul.* The piece is in AABA song form, the most commonly used form in American songwriting in this century and something we should probably all know about. It consists of a main strain, A; that strain repeated exactly (or almost exactly); then the B melody (called the release, the middle, the bridge, or the channel), typically in a different key; then back to A. Each strain is eight bars, therefore we have what is called thirty-two bar AABA popular song form. From this album, *Sweethearts on Parade, Moten Swing, The Man I Love, Too Marvelous for Words, When Lights are Low,* and many others all use this AABA form, even though some of them are not songs; that is, they are not meant to be sung.

Pieces like *You'd Be So Nice to Come Home To, Wrappin' It Up, Embraceable You,* and *I Should Care* are based on another commonly used thirty-two bar structure, usually described as ABAB or sometimes ABAC.

In the Goodman Trio's *Body and Soul,* pianist Teddy Wilson's first solo is the bridge of the first AABA chorus, and basically he uses the song's original B melody. But his second solo (AA in the second chorus) is a brilliant invention, a beautiful *new* melody, with no thematic relationship to the original at all.

The same would be true of every solo after the opening in Goodman's *I Found a New Baby*: all are new melodies, made up spontaneously by the players, oriented in the harmony of the piece and only fleetingly in its melody.

Sometimes jazzmen start inventing from the very beginning of a performance, with no opening interpretation of a theme. Brilliant examples of such improvising in this collection are Coleman Hawkins's *Body and Soul* and Charlie Parker's *Embraceable You.*

"The melody" in such performances is, of course, whatever the player is playing. As we know, it may be quite like its familiar point of departure, or only something like it, or (melodically speaking) nothing whatever like the

Billie Holiday, Lester Young, Coleman Hawkins, and Gerry Mulligan in the 1957 CBS tv special "The Sound of Jazz." (CBS Special Products)

original. And it is improvised. If we know that a music, a piece of theater, or any work of art is being improvised, made up for us as we listen to it or watch it, we participate in it emotionally in a special way. But in the final analysis, an improvisation must stand or fall on how good it is. The remarkable thing about jazz is that its best players produce such good instrumental music spontaneously.

As one digs more deeply into jazz solos, one comes to realize that their melodies often have a most intricate, subtle, and delightful sense of pattern and design to them. Obviously, a good jazz solo isn't just a matter of stringing musical phrases together to fit a predetermined chord sequence. The comments below on such solos as Louis Armstrong's *Struttin' with Some Barbecue,* Teddy Wilson's *Body and Soul,* Count Basie's and Lester Young's *Doggin' Around,* Charlie Christian's solos, Charlie Parker's two versions of *Embraceable You,* Thelonious Monk's blues improvisation on *Bag's Groove,* and Ornette Coleman's *Congeniality* will particularly serve to introduce the listener to such delights.

New Pieces from Old

Not only do jazz musicians constantly make up new melodies extemporaneously on established outlines (or chord progressions), they also *write* new opening themes using familiar chord changes as a guide. Thus, in this album *Moten Swing* takes its structure from a popular song by Walter Donaldson called *You're Driving Me Crazy*. If you know *You're Driving Me Crazy*, put on *Moten Swing* and sing along with it and you'll see. Similarly, the Duke Ellington piece *In a Mellotone* borrows the outline but not the melody of *Rose Room*. Again, sing along and you'll see. In a somewhat subtler way, the Thelonious Monk piece *Evidence* uses the song *Just You, Just Me.*

The ultimate point in turning *You're Driving Me Crazy* into *Moten Swing* is, of course, to gain a more jazzlike instrumental setting for the performance than the original melody might offer.

One can gain a minor education in the use of *I Got Rhythm* just through this collection. Don Byas's *I Got Rhythm* is an obvious starting place, for both his use of the original melody and his departures from it. But the Count Basie--Lester Young *Lester Leaps In* is also *I Got Rhythm* harmonically, and so is Dizzy Gillespie's *Shaw 'Nuff.*

The foregoing should not make jazz seem a musical guessing game. The point is to acquaint the listener with common practices in jazz that he may want to listen for. But in the final analysis, a jazz musician's melody is whatever he is playing, regardless of what he may be using as a guide or point of departure. No one is *required* to hear the chord progression of *Willow Weep for Me* when listening to *Taxi War Dance*. There is, however, one progression, one outline, one structure, that all Americans ought to be thoroughly familiar with: the blues.

Hearing the Blues

The best basic example of the blues, and the best place for the listener to start in this album, is Bessie Smith's *Lost Your Head Blues*. All the following selections are also, in whole or in part, regular twelve-bar blues:

Bessie Smith—*St. Louis Blues*
King Oliver—*Dippermouth Blues*
Jelly Roll Morton—*Dead Man Blues*
Sidney Bechet—*Blue Horizon*
Louis Armstrong—*West End Blues*
Meade "Lux" Lewis—*Honky Tonk Train*
Charlie Christian—*Breakfast Feud*
Duke Ellington—*Ko-Ko*
Charlie Parker—*Parker's Mood*
Thelonious Monk—*Misterioso*
Thelonious Monk—blues improvisation from *Bag's Groove*
Wes Montgomery—*West Coast Blues*.

In addition, Duke Ellington's *Blue Serge* is an ingenious treatment of the eight-bar blues. And Dexter Gordon's *Bikini* is in the blues variant that adds an eight-bar bridge (12-12-8-12).

Probably the easiest way to begin to get the blues in one's ear, so that recognizing the form will become almost second nature, is to try singing some favorite vocal blues choruses along with some instrumental blues recordings; for example, sing the words to Bessie Smith's *Lost Your Head* along with Bechet's *Blue Horizon*. Incidentally, both *Blue Horizon* and the *Honky Tonk Train* are particularly helpful to the nonmusical beginner, since both Bechet and Lewis tend to end each of their choruses with a recurring idea.

A lot can be gained, also, by simply counting off blues choruses. Since most jazz is in 4/4 (or *said* to be in 4/4, at any rate), and since the blues chorus is a brief one, counting to four twelve times, on the beats, while listening to how the cadences fall, will cover a blues chorus.

The blues in this album represent a succinct view of a remarkable cultural achievement. Within less than a score of years, the form had inspired Bechet's and Parker's personal statements, the complex orchestral textures of Ellington's *Ko-Ko,* and the perceptive instrumental structure of Monk's *Misterioso.*

Hearing the Whole

If a music is at least partly improvised, made up for us as we listen to it, what part does a composer play in it? And what does a jazz arranger do when he works up a popular song, let us say, for a group of musicians to play and improvise on?

This collection contains a number of performances that were chosen for their composition and their overall formal accomplishments. Among them are:

Jelly Roll Morton—*Dead Man Blues* and *Black Bottom Stomp*
Fletcher Henderson—*Wrappin' It Up*
Duke Ellington—several pieces, but particularly *Ko-Ko,*
    Concerto for Cootie, and *Blue Serge*
Thelonious Monk—particularly *Misterioso,* and *Evidence*
Modern Jazz Quartet—*Django*
Sonny Rollins—*Blue 7.*

The comments below, on the individual selections, should serve as a guide toward hearing each of those performances whole.

Other Qualities

Besides learning to hear jazz melody, learning to recognize the blues, and listening for formal and compositional virtues, a listener can approach the records in other ways.

For example, the evolution of jazz trumpet style from King Oliver to Louis Armstrong to Roy Eldridge to Dizzy Gillespie can be heard, as can its further evolution to Miles Davis, Theodore "Fats" Navarro, and Clifford Brown. Armstrong's own growth can be studied, and (particularly because of his early association with Charlie Parker), so can Davis's.

Oliver's muted work can be heard for its effect on James "Bubber"

Miley with Ellington, and then Miley's on Cootie Williams—and on the whole texture of Ellington's music.

Coleman Hawkins's early days through his maturity can be traced, as can the work of his tenor saxophone "pupils," Ben Webster and Don Byas. Then there are the innovations of Lester Young and the remarkable synthesis of the two parent styles of Hawkins and Young that was made by Dexter Gordon, and the further developments by Sonny Rollins and John Coltrane.

Then there are comparisons that can be made on such things as our three versions of *Body and Soul* or on many examples of players improvising on the blues or the *I Got Rhythm* chord progression.

A collection like this one inevitably presents highlights. If every selection cannot be a masterpiece, then it is at least an outstanding recording, or it displays work by an outstanding musician. But as every teacher knows, bad examples, or at least honest efforts that fail, can be as instructive as good ones. Take, for example, the sometimes difficult question of swing. There are many successful players—a few of them otherwise admirable—who have problems with swing or even who do not swing at all. Pianist Lennie Tristano for example, although he was an excellent improviser and a musician whose sense of tempo was always nearly perfect, did not swing in the manner of his fellow players of the late forties and early fifties.

For the alert and sympathetic listener, there are things to be learned from the occasional flaws in these recordings; for instance, the obvious rhythmic contrast between the players with a slightly older New Orleans feel for rhythm and the innovative Armstrong on *Struttin' with Some Barbecue*; the superiority of Hines and Armstrong to the other participants on *West End Blues*; the sloppiness of Armstrong's accompanists on *Sweethearts on Parade* (which does not deter him in his glorious statement at all), particularly the awkwardly unswinging alto break that precedes his trumpet chorus after the vocal; the immaturity of young Eddie Heywood's piano style on Coleman Hawkins's *The Man I Love*.

The Trumbauer-Beiderbecke recordings are particularly uneven, in ways that will be addressed in the notes on the selections below. Critic André Hodeir has complained of the drumming on Ellington's *Ko-Ko*. Clearly, the pianist on Dexter Gordon's *Bikini* is not swinging, but, just as clearly, that is because he was not quite prepared for the blues in minor and was still looking for the chord changes when someone called for a take—a shortcoming that does not restrain Gordon in the least.

There are other occasional imperfections, as is inevitable in a spontaneous music like jazz, and some of them will be noted below—again, not to point the finger but because an awareness of them enables us to participate more deeply in the music and in its essential humanity.

Two books that should prove particularly helpful in using any of the above basic approaches to the music are Leonard Feather's *The Book of Jazz* and my own *Where's the Melody? A Listener's Introduction to Jazz*.

The Recordings

All selections recorded in New York City except where noted.

RECORD SIDE 1
CASSETTE SIDE A
CD I

SCOTT JOPLIN
Maple Leaf Rag
(Mus., Scott Joplin)
Roll made by Scott Joplin, 4/16. Recorded in stereo 6/1/86 from Connorized piano roll #10265 played on 1910 Steinway upright with footpump and double tracker bar. Engineer, Ken Glaza. Roll lent by Michael Montgomery. Included through the courtesy of QRS Music Rolls, Buffalo, NY.

A player piano is a mechanical thing. It reproduces no dynamics and few nuances of touch or shading. Every note is struck mechanically, with the same pressure as every other note. And piano roll manufacturers would sometimes doctor a roll—punch in extra embellishments and effects—after a performer had made it, often producing a result that would have been impossible for any pianist to play alone.

Yet Joplin's piano rolls are the only evidence we have of the way he performed his rags and are more authentic in their way than anyone else's version. If one makes certain aural allowances, they are good evidence. Historically, rolls were one way Joplin's music spread, and many young pianists learned to play by placing their fingers on the keys as they went down.

With one minor difference, and with a slightly doctored bass at a couple of points, Joplin here performs the keenly structured *Maple Leaf Rag*, as it was published, with its fine contrasting themes and their repeats (AABBACCDD).

Bessie Smith.

JELLY ROLL MORTON
Maple Leaf Rag
(Mus., Scott Joplin)
Rec. 6/38, Washington, DC.
Jelly Roll Morton (p).
Recorded for the Library of Congress. First issue Circle 22; portion of mx 1654A. Included through the courtesy of the estate of Anita Ford.

Recorded on an inexpensive portable disc recorder (and originally interrupted at one point for a change of blank acetate discs), Ferdinand "Jelly Roll" Morton's transformation of *Maple Leaf Rag* into New Orleans style is one of the most revealing examples of that city's contribution to jazz. It is immediately evident that the basis of the contribution was rhythmic. Morton embellishes the piece two-handedly, with a swinging introduction (borrowed from the ending of the A strain) followed by ABACCDD (with a hint of the tango in the first D and a real New Orleans stomp variation in the second). In accordance with his belief that piano styles should follow band styles, Morton is here clearly playing a trumpet-clarinet part with his right hand and a trombone-rhythm part with his left.

BESSIE SMITH
St. Louis Blues
(Mus. & lyr., W.C. Handy)
Rec. 1/14/25.
Bessie Smith (voc); Louis Armstrong (c); Fred Longshaw (reed organ).
First issue Columbia 14064-D; mx 140241-1. Included through the courtesy of CBS Special Products.

This performance displays the restrained yet powerful collaboration of three major talents: composer, singer, and cornetist-trumpeter. Handy's contributions are here exemplified in his most famous piece. He adopted a raglike structure to build indigenous material into a fine vocal piece in three themes, AA (a twelve-measure blues and its repeat), BB (sixteen measures—this section is often played as a tango), and C (the main twelve-measure blues section).

Bessie Smith's interpretation gains noticeably from her repeated distillation and simplification of Handy's melodies to suit her own vocal and emotional resources. And Fred Longshaw's allusions to a country church organ style suit the mood superbly.

"When I was a little girl," the great gospel singer Mahalia Jackson once said of Bessie Smith's recordings, "I felt she was having troubles like me. That's why it was such a comfort for the people of the South to hear her. She expressed something they couldn't put into words."

And so she did also for all sorts of people everywhere.

BESSIE SMITH
Lost Your Head Blues
(Mus. & lyr., Bessie Smith)
Rec. 5/4/26.
Bessie Smith (voc); Joe Smith (c); Fletcher Henderson (p).
First issue Columbia 14158-D; mx 142149-1. Included through the courtesy of CBS Special Products.

This informal collaboration is perhaps even more revealing of Bessie Smith's talent than the preceding. The story goes (and it could well be true) that she simply ad libbed *Lost Your Head Blues* in the studio to fill out a record date that had come out one selection short. She preferred the subdued lyricism of Joe Smith as a collaborator to the more powerful Armstrong, and certainly the interplay here of poetry, voice, and accompaniment is remarkable.

There is nothing quite like the climactic effect of the way Smith here sings "Days are lonesome, nights are so long," even in her own recordings. The effect is of a totally emotional statement, but it is one that cannot be achieved without a singular vocal discipline and self-knowledge.

In the 1970s Smith's Columbia recordings were awarded the honor of being reissued complete. It is almost unfair to single out individual selections, but we will risk recommending *Young Woman's Blues*, much admired for its ironic poetry; *Backwater Blues*; her exemplary transformation of the popular song *After You've Gone*; and *Jailhouse Blues*.

KING OLIVER'S CREOLE JAZZ BAND
Dippermouth Blues

(Mus., Joe Oliver)
Rec. 4/6/23, Richmond, IN
King Oliver, Louis Armstrong (c); Honoré
Dutrey (tb); Johnny Dodds (cl); Lil Hardin (p);
Bill Johnson (bj, voc break); Baby Dodds (d).
Soloists: Dodds; Oliver.
First issue Gennett 5132; mx 11389-B. In-
cluded through the courtesy of Fantasy Rec-
ords.

This is our first sample of the dense
polyphonic style of the New Orleans
ensemble, performed by one of the great
New Orleans groups.

The King Oliver band was a collection
of individuals who knew each other's
ways so well that a group improvisation
was possible by a kind of spontaneous
reflex. This instrumental blues features
ensemble passages and the anguished-
joyous solos of Johnny Dodds (two choruses) and a skillfully wa-wa muted King
Oliver (three choruses). These solos
became so identified with *Dippermouth*
(and with the version called *Sugarfoot
Stomp* to which Don Redman added a
sixteen-bar secondary theme) that other
soloists would reproduce them, sometimes note for note, when performing it.
Indeed, imitating Oliver's choruses became a stop-gap for uninspired trumpeters when playing the blues in C or B-flat
well into the 1940s.

We hear indications of a musical leadership to come in the ensemble chorus
between the two solos, where the lead
is played by Louis Armstrong, not Oliver. The recorded sound here is not up
to the general standards even of 1923,
but the performance repays careful dig-
ging and listening.

Clarinetist Garvin Bushell once said of
the Oliver band, "I was very impressed
with their blues and their sound. The
trumpets and clarinets in the East had a
better 'legitimate' quality, but their
sound touched you more. It was...more
expressive of how the people felt....The
Dodds brothers...felt very highly about
what they were playing as though they
knew they were doing something nobody else could do. I'd say they did regard themselves as artists...."

JELLY ROLL MORTON'S RED HOT PEPPERS
Black Bottom Stomp

(Mus., Jelly Roll Morton)
Rec. 9/15/26, Chicago.
Jelly Roll Morton (p); George Mitchell (t);
Edward "Kid" Ory (tb); Omer Simeon (cl);
Johnny St. Cyr (bj); John Lindsay (b); Andrew
Hilaire (d).
Soloists: Mitchell; Simeon; Morton; Mitchell;
St. Cyr; Ory.
First issue Victor 20221; mx 36239-2. Included
through the courtesy of RCA Records.

Morton's records deserve the most
careful formal scrutiny, and *Black Bottom Stomp* is one of his best compositions, orchestrations, and recordings.

The performance begins with an extended introduction. Then the ensemble,
with the clarinet much in evidence,
states Morton's opening, sixteen-
measure theme. For a second chorus on
that same theme, the trumpet and ensemble exchange rapid four-measure
phrases. In the final chorus of the opening theme, the clarinet solos, accompanied only by the banjo.

Following an interlude that changes
key, Morton has the horns state his second, twenty-measure theme in counterpoint. In the middle, there is a "break"
(the rhythm section suspends its accompaniment for two measures) which
is shared by the trumpet and trombone.
We then hear an improvised clarinet
solo for one chorus, during which the
black bottom rhythm (a slight variant of
the Charleston) is very strong. Morton
himself takes over for a piano solo
which is played unaccompanied. Next,
the trumpet improvises over stop-
time—where the beat is only intermittently stated. Then a banjo solo. Then
the ensemble in a very light, improvised
counterpoint (with a humorous two-bar
cymbal break in the middle). Then the
ensemble for the final chorus, stronger
now, with fine accents from the string
bass and the drummer's tom-tom, and a
surprise break by the trombone.

Such a brief description is apt to
make Morton's recording sound over-
loaded, cluttered, even a bit pretentious.
Actually, it flows from beginning to end

with a sprightly, imaginative, yet unassuming musical logic and wit that anyone can enjoy—and that a sophisticated listener may miss.

JELLY ROLL MORTON'S RED HOT PEPPERS
Dead Man Blues [dialogue deleted]
(Mus., Jelly Roll Morton)
Rec. 9/21/26, Chicago.
Jelly Roll Morton (p); George Mitchell (t); Edward "Kid" Ory (tb); Barney Bigard, Darnell Howard, Omer Simeon (cl); Johnny St. Cyr (bj); John Lindsay (b); Andrew Hilaire (d).
Soloists: Simeon; Mitchell; Ory.
First issue Victor 20252; mx 36284-1. Included through the courtesy of RCA Records.

Morton's arrangement here begins with Kid Ory's trombone leading Chopin's funeral march (a theme also used in the hymn *Flee As a Bird*) with just a hint of the breathy, ironic humor that is always buried deep in *Dead Man Blues*.

The opening ensemble on the first theme of the piece is a lovely version of New Orleans polyphonic style—intricate, restrained, and delicate—followed by Omer Simeon's clarinet variation. Morton's second theme is stated only in George Mitchell's trumpet variation of two continuous choruses. The rifflike third theme enters, stated in simple harmony by the three clarinets. In the next chorus the clarinets do an exact repeat of what they have just played, and the trombone improvises a beautiful, simple, melancholy theme in counterpoint. This two-part counterpoint leads logically to the next chorus, a three-part, improvised counterpoint among the three main horns, which returns to the opening theme. Thus this final chorus, balancing the opening, is both a partial recapitulation and a beautifully understated climax.

JELLY ROLL MORTON'S RED HOT PEPPERS
Grandpa's Spells
(Mus., Jelly Roll Morton)
Rec. 12/16/26, Chicago.
Jelly Roll Morton (p); George Mitchell (t); Edward "Kid" Ory (tb); Omer Simeon (cl); Johnny St. Cyr (g, bj); John Lindsay (b); Andrew Hilaire (d).
Soloists: St. Cyr; Mitchell; Morton; Simeon; Ory; Lindsay; Ory; Lindsay; Mitchell; Simeon; Morton; Simeon; St. Cyr.
First issue Bluebird B-10254; mx 37255-2. Included through the courtesy of RCA Records.

Grandpa's Spells is a superb example of Jelly Roll Morton's perceptive, individual use of the New Orleans style. The piece is in three sections, structurally (but not rhythmically or emotionally) a late ragtime composition.

It was also originally a piano piece, but in this rendering for eight instruments, Morton has used all eight in po-

lyphony. Then he has juxtaposed trumpet and rhythm, and to vary that texture and timbre, he has used muted trumpet and rhythm; trombone and string bass; string bass unaccompanied; guitar unaccompanied; piano, banjo, and drums (with no bass). In addition, there are short breaks, full solos, a range of dynamics.

The general outline is: Introduction/A/ A^1/B/B^1/A^2/C/C^1/C^2/C^3/Coda (ending), and the listener is invited to hear how each of the above listed combination of instruments and textures is used in each treatment of each theme.

The performance is also evidence of Morton's understanding that a simple assignment of a piano score to instruments would not work very well. In the early published version, the opening theme (here given to the guitar) begins:

And the trio (here given to the trumpet, then the clarinet) begins:

TRIO

Crash
(Strike bass open handed)

Crash

JELLY ROLL MORTON
King Porter Stomp
(Mus., Jelly Roll Morton)
Rec. 12/14/39.
Jelly Roll Morton (p).
First issue General 4005; mx R-2565. Included through the courtesy of Commodore Records.

Morton's *King Porter Stomp* was his hit and, with its three sections cut back to two, a staple piece for the swing bands of the 1930s. This recording, made late in Morton's life during a brief period of his rediscovery, is the best and most energetic of his several versions. (Oddly, he never recorded the piece with a full New Orleans ensemble.)

King Porter is in three sixteen-measure sections, and Morton plays it with no returns: Introduction/A/A^1/B/B^1/ Interlude/C/C^1/C^2/ and a shortened (twelve-measure) C^3.

Those C sections form the robust climax of *King Porter*, where Morton really shows off his capacity for structured, building, thematic variations, and (undoubtedly because of its riff-like melodic material) the section that most attracted the big swing bands.

RECORD SIDE 2

RED ONION JAZZ BABIES
Cake Walking Babies from Home
(Mus. & lyr., Clarence Williams, Chris Smith, Henry Troy)
Rec. 12/22/24.
Louis Armstrong (c); Sidney Bechet (ss); Charlie Irvis (tb); Lil Armstrong (p); Buddy Christian (bj); Alberta Hunter and Clarence Todd, as "Beatty and Todd" (voc).
Soloists: Louis Armstrong; Bechet; Irvis; Bechet.
First issue Gennett 5627; mx 9248-A. Included through the courtesy of Fantasy Records.

There are Louis Armstrong solos on King Oliver recordings, but he first began to shine as a soloist after he left his early mentor, and particularly when he joined Fletcher Henderson's orchestra in New York and began freelance recording on the side as well.

This assemblage, named for the Red Onion, a New Orleans bar, joined Armstrong with the outstandingly talented Bechet, who was already well established internationally as a musician's musician. Bechet had absorbed the early New Orleans innovations and arrived at a point in his development comparable to the young Armstrong's. A clarinetist, Bechet had also adopted the soprano saxophone and formed a style on it based not only on the clarinet's obbligato role but also on the trumpet's lead.

All of this serves to set up a marvelous, healthy competitive tension in this sweeping performance, particularly in the last two choruses.

The cakewalk dance of the title actually dates back even before ragtime, and the vocal duet here is also decidedly old-fashioned in style. Trombonist Charlie Irvis is not quite in touch with Armstrong's and Bechet's innovative rhythmic ideas, but the performance otherwise—the inventive swing of the principals; their inventive interplay, with its exchanges of the lead instrument; the suspenseful breaks, climaxed by a stop-time episode by each man—these things were ahead of their time in 1924, and they are timeless.

Incidentally, a couple of weeks later, virtually this same group recorded this same piece for Okeh Records under the name Clarence Williams' Blue Five. The results (which slightly favored Armstrong) make an instructive comparison.

SIDNEY BECHET AND HIS BLUE NOTE JAZZ MEN
Blue Horizon

(Mus., Sidney Bechet)
Rec. 12/20/44.
Sidney Bechet (cl); Sidney De Paris (t); Vic Dickenson (tb); Art Hodes (p); George "Pops" Foster (b); Manzie Johnson (d).
Soloist: Bechet.
First issue Blue Note 43; mx BN 208. Included through the courtesy of Capitol Records.

Since Bechet's favorite instrument was the soprano saxophone, it is ironic that this beautiful, and beautifully paced, slow blues improvisation was done on clarinet.

A performance like this one speaks for itself, but one should not assume that Bechet was capable only of such personal extensions of the New Orleans idiom. On one of his last (and best) recording dates, he was performing pieces like *The Man I Love* and *Rose Room* with Martial Solal, then the most accomplished young pianist of France.

JAMES P. JOHNSON
Carolina Shout

(Mus., James P. Johnson)
Rec. 10/18/21.
James P. Johnson (p).
First issue Okeh 4495; mx 70260-C. Included through the courtesy of CBS Special Products.

Johnson has been called the father of stride piano, the northeastern development out of ragtime; his associates and followers included Willie "the Lion" Smith, Fats Waller, Duke Ellington, Count Basie—even Art Tatum—and (once removed) Thelonious Monk.

None of the early stride men were really blues men (although, of course, they all played pieces in blues form) and perhaps that is why the paths they took out of the rhythmic and emotional limitations of ragtime were so different from those of the New Orleans men.

Carolina Shout (a "shout" was a ringshout, a celebrative and originally religious Negro dance) became a test piece. Both Smith and Waller played and recorded it, and the young Ellington learned it by following a Johnson piano roll set at slow speed.

Structurally a three-theme rag, *Carolina Shout* is, as Gunther Schuller observes in *Early Jazz*, more linear and percussive than melodic, and broken up with tricky, shifting rhythmic patterns. Listen to Johnson's left hand during the first eight bars of the first theme, and then during the second eight, for instance.

LOUIS ARMSTRONG AND HIS HOT FIVE
Big Butter and Egg Man from the West [abridged]

(Mus. & lyr., Louis Armstrong, Percy Venable)
Rec. 11/16/26, Chicago.
Louis Armstrong (c); Edward "Kid" Ory (tb); Johnny Dodds (cl); Lil Armstrong (p); Johnny St. Cyr (bj).
Soloists: Lil Armstrong; Louis Armstrong.
First issue Okeh 8423; mx 9892-A. Included through the courtesy of CBS Special Products.

Armstrong's solo on *Big Butter and Egg Man* (the expression means a small-time big-spender) is one of his most praised, most celebrated, and most imitated. André Hodeir singled it out in *Jazz: Its Evolution and Essence,* saying "it is impossible to imagine anything more sober and balanced," and Gunther Schuller in *Early Jazz* said that "no composer, not even a Mozart or a Schubert, composed anything more natural and simply inspired."

This edited version presents the classic instrumental portions of a recording that otherwise included some verbal bantering and a vocal chorus (not by Louis), which do not stand up to repeated hearings. Lil Armstrong was Louis's wife at the time.

CASSETTE SIDE B

LOUIS ARMSTRONG AND HIS HOT SEVEN
Potato Head Blues
(Mus., Louis Armstrong)
Rec. 5/10/27, Chicago.
Louis Armstrong (c); John Thomas (tb); Johnny Dodds (cl); Lil Armstrong (p); Johnny St. Cyr (bj); Pete Briggs (tba); Baby Dodds (d).
Soloists: Louis Armstrong; J. Dodds; St. Cyr; Louis Armstrong.
First issue Okeh 8503; mx 80855-C. Included through the courtesy of CBS Special Products.

The stop-time (in effect, an extended series of two-bar breaks) of Louis Armstrong's *Potato Head* has been described by Richard Hadlock in *Jazz Masters of the Twenties* as "a triumph of subtle syncopation and rhythmic enlightenment; strong accents on weak beats and whole phrases placed *against* rather than *on* the pulse create delightful tension. This tension is then suddenly released with an incisive on-the-beat figure, which in turn leads into more tension-building devices. Thus does Armstrong build the emotional pitch of the solo over a full chorus."

Armstrong's climactic solo is well prepared for, from the opening ensemble through his first solo—a relatively casual interpretation of *Potato Head*'s rarely played verse—through Johnny Dodds's strong, energetic solo which returns to the piece's main section.

LOUIS ARMSTRONG AND HIS HOT FIVE
Struttin' with Some Barbecue
(Mus., Lillian Hardin Armstrong)
Rec. 12/9/27, Chicago.
Louis Armstrong (c); Edward "Kid" Ory (tb); Johnny Dodds (cl); Lil Armstrong (p); Johnny St. Cyr (bj).
Soloists: Dodds; Ory; Louis Armstrong.
First issue Okeh 8566; mx 82037-B. Included through the courtesy of CBS Special Products.

Armstrong's story on records between 1923 and 1932 is one of almost continuous sweeping growth—and after that is frequently one of entrenched excellence.

The Hot Five and Hot Seven were studio-assembled groups (not assembled by the leader), mostly of New Orleans musicians with whom Armstrong had previously worked. But Armstrong the master soloist is clearly breaking through the old formulas, and the Armstrong solo on *Struttin' With Some Barbecue* captures the inventive, melodious improvisor at a peak. Richard Hadlock describes this solo as "a radiant experiment in the construction of long lines without sacrifice of melodic simplicity and rhythmic momentum." Also noteworthy is Johnny St. Cyr's work, which shows a grasp of the implications of Armstrong's innovations.

LOUIS ARMSTRONG AND HIS HOT FIVE
Hotter Than That
(Mus., Lillian Hardin Armstrong)
Rec. 12/13/27, Chicago.
Louis Armstrong (c, voc); Edward "Kid" Ory (tb); Johnny Dodds (cl); Lil Armstrong (p); Johnny St. Cyr (bj); Lonnie Johnson (g).
Soloists: Louis Armstrong (c); Dodds; Louis Armstrong (voc) and Johnson; Lil Armstrong; Ory; Louis Armstrong (c).
First issue Okeh 8535; mx 82055-B. Included through the courtesy of CBS Special Products.

The bursting vitality of *Hotter Than That,* which gains greatly from Lonnie Johnson's addition to the ensemble, is "a fitting tour de force climax" to the original Hot Five series of recordings, according to Hadlock. He adds, "Only the necessity for breathing appears to have prevented Armstrong...from execut-

Louis Armstrong in the star years of the 1930s. *(Duncan Schiedt Collection)*

ing whole choruses at a time as long unbroken single statements." The description might refer to Armstrong's scat (wordless) vocal improvising as well as his horn.

The recurring two-bar break adds to the heat of the performance—and it comes in the momentous *middle* of a chorus rather than at the beginning or end.

Gunther Schuller suggests that the overall scheme and arrangement of *Hotter Than That* by Don Redman is almost as commendable as the innovative solo work and interplay. Armstrong's brilliance has, momentarily at least, found a worthy framework, and a fine companion in guitarist Johnson.

LOUIS ARMSTRONG AND HIS HOT FIVE
West End Blues

(Mus., Joe Oliver & Clarence Williams)
Rec. 6/28/28, Chicago.
Louis Armstrong (t, voc); Fred Robinson (tb); Jimmy Strong (cl); Earl Hines (p); Mancy Cara (bj); Zutty Singleton (d).
Soloists: Armstrong (t); Robinson; Armstrong (voc) and Strong; Hines; Armstrong (t); Hines.
First issue Okeh 8597; mx 400967-B. Included through the courtesy of CBS Special Products.

With *West End Blues* we leap forward, not into the next decade and a half, when Armstrong's major innovations would dominate the music, but even beyond that, for he here introduces ideas of phrasing and melodic rhythm that lay neglected until the arrival of Charlie Parker in the 1940s. Further, we find Armstrong now in the company of Earl Hines, who was not only Armstrong's counterpart on piano but an inspiration to him as well.

Armstrong's opening and closing choruses on *West End Blues* are a kind of continuum in which shining virtuosity and grandiose simplicity are in perfect balance. The dazzling introduction fades into a theme statement that is almost an understatement until it builds to the rising triplet figures of its final two bars. And in the final chorus, Armstrong picks up the concluding high B-flat of his first chorus, holds it passionately for almost

four measures, and leads to virtuoso descending phrases, as though to balance his opening.

Armstrong has here taken the idea of simple double-timing (which he used so well at this period on the blues called *Muggles*) and carried it into a still newer and more complex kind of rhythmic thinking.

RECORD SIDE 3

LOUIS ARMSTRONG AND EARL HINES
Weather Bird

(Mus., Joe Oliver)
Rec. 12/5/28, Chicago.
Louis Armstrong (t); Earl Hines (p).
First issue Okeh 41454; mx 402199-A. Included through the courtesy of CBS Special Products.

This mounting, unencumbered duet, which is based on a piece Armstrong had recorded in 1923 with the Oliver band, is the fullest statement on record of his encounter with Hines. Their treatment of the piece's third section, with Hines's substitute chord, is particularly exhilarating. Only *Skip the Gutter* approaches *Weather Bird* as an expression of the collaborative, creative rivalry of these two men. In comparing this recording with the Oliver version, one is astounded to realize how far these two men brought jazz improvisation in a mere five years.

LOUIS ARMSTRONG AND HIS ORCHESTRA
Sweethearts on Parade

(Mus., Carmen Lombardo; lyr., Charles Newman)
Rec. 12/23/30, Los Angeles.
Louis Armstrong (t, voc); George Orendorff, Harold Scott (t); Luther Graven (tb); Les Hite (as, bar, ldr); Marvin Johnson (as); Charlie Jones (cl, ts); Henry Prince (p); Bill Perkins (bj, g); Joe Bailey (b); Lionel Hampton (d).
Soloist: Armstrong.
First issue Columbia 2688-D; mx 404417-A. Included through the courtesy of CBS Special Products.

Armstrong by this time had become a well-known popular figure with a wide and growing audience. Partly as a consequence, he had moved away from the traditional twelve- and sixteen-measure structures and undertaken also the popular songs of the time, some of them quite sentimental, to say the least.

Armstrong begins his opening chorus in Sweethearts on Parade *so obliquely off the melody that one gets the effect of an introduction and opening statement all in one. Indeed, he seems almost to be tossing random asymmetrical phrases in the air until a particular phrase comes along that somehow ties the previous phrases together. And when he does, allow us to glimpse the melody, he quickly veers away from it again into inventions of his own, usually complex ones that dance around the beat and offer hints of what is to come. After the vocal, a repeated blues-inspired paraphrase of the song's opening idea...leads to a deliberately earth-bound, drumlike phrase, thence to his flying interpolation of the motive of the* High Society *obbligato (here is where Charlie Parker must have gotten that favorite lick). From this point to the end of the chorus, we are once again into a kind of rhythmic thinking that was innovative even for Armstrong.*

Sweethearts on Parade, *then, is built up in brief, intriguing but ultimately logical fragments.* (Martin Williams, *The Jazz Tradition*).

LOUIS ARMSTRONG AND HIS ORCHESTRA
I Gotta Right to Sing the Blues [dialogue deleted]
(Mus., Harold Arlen; lyr., Ted Koehler) Arr., Zilner Randolph. Rec. 1/26/33, Chicago. Louis Armstrong (t, voc); Zilner Randolph, Ellis Whitlock (tr); Keg Johnson (tb); Scoville Brown, George Oldham (cl, as); "Budd" Johnson (cl, ts); Teddy Wilson (p); Mike McKendrick (bj, g); Bill Oldham (b); Yank Porter (d).
Soloists: Armstrong (voc) and Brown (cl); Armstrong (t).
First issue Victor 24233; mx 74892-1. Included through the courtesy of RCA Records.

Armstrong's final trumpet chorus on *I Gotta Right to Sing the Blues* is one of his most grand and eloquent transformations of a popular song. It is in a mature ballad style, free of almost all his usual rhythmic embellishments and ornamentations. It seems to float above the tempo, above the meter, above the piece itself. It gains its most telling effects from a simplification of Harold Arlen's melody—and a good popular melody it is. (But that might not matter to an artist like Armstrong: hear his passionate recomposition of a decidedly poor theme in *That's My Home*.)

Incidentally, this Armstrong version had a specific and instructive influence on Billie Holiday's treatment of the song.

FRANKIE TRUMBAUER AND HIS ORCHESTRA
Singin' the Blues
(Mus., Jimmy McHugh; lyr., Dorothy Fields) Rec. 2/4/27.
Bix Beiderbecke (c); Frankie Trumbauer (C-melody sax); Bill Rank (tb); Jimmy Dorsey (cl, as); Paul Mertz (p); Eddie Lang (g); Chauncey Morehouse (d).
Soloists: Trumbauer, Beiderbecke; Dorsey (cl); Lang.
First issue Okeh 40772; mx 80393-B. Included through the courtesy of CBS Special Products.

Riverboat Shuffle
(Mus., Hoagy Carmichael; lyr., Irving Mills & Mitchell Parish) Rec. 5/9/27.
Bix Beiderbecke (c); Bill Rank (tb); Don Murray (cl, bars); Frankie Trumbauer (C-melody sax); Doc Ryker (as); Itzy Riskin (p); Eddie Lang (g); Chauncey Morehouse (d).
Soloists: Lang; Riskin; Murray (cl); Beiderbecke; Rank; Murray (cl); Beiderbecke; Murray (cl); Lang; Trumbauer.
First issue Okeh 40822; mx 81072-B. Included through the courtesy of CBS Special Products.

Louis Armstrong said that when he heard young Bix Beiderbecke he realized that they were both working on the same thing, and by that he presumably meant on making jazz a soloist's art. Yet Beiderbecke's fragile, lyric sensibilities were almost opposite to Armstrong's robust statements.

Beiderbecke has been called the first white jazz musician whose work can be

taken seriously. His life has been romanticized along a kind of Keatsian-sacrificial pattern (he was dead before he was out of his twenties). His recordings under his own name and Trumbauer's survive almost solely on the basis of his lovely sound and his imaginative solos. Most of them were made by contingents from the Paul Whiteman orchestra with which he played, and several of the other participants have trouble with swing and trouble escaping from the jazzy clichés of the day.

Riverboat Shuffle, interestingly written as a kind of up-to-date version of an early New Orleans piece, has Beiderbecke's strong lead in its opening and closing, a good cornet break, and a fine solo which is a true invention, not an embellishment or paraphrase. That approach was typical of Bix's work.

Singin' the Blues is better overall, and it was an influential recording. Rex Stewart, on Fletcher Henderson's recording of the piece, reproduced Bix's solo, as did several others. And Lester Young used to carry a copy of Trumbauer's *Singin' the Blues* around in his saxophone case, explaining, "They were telling some stories that I liked to hear."

Also contributing to both performances here is guitarist Eddie Lang. His "time" (ability to keep a steady tempo) is a bit shaky, but his sympathy is self-evident and his harmonic knowledge had its influence.

Beiderbecke's was an authentic talent that, in its way, touched nearly everyone who played jazz in the twenties and thirties.

JIMMIE NOONE'S APEX CLUB ORCHESTRA
Four or Five Times
(Mus., Byron Gay; lyr., Marco H. Hellman)
Rec. 5/16/28.
Jimmie Noone (cl, voc); Joe Poston (as, voc); Earl Hines (p); Bud Scott (bj, g); Johnny Wells (d).
Soloists: Hines; Noone and Poston (voc).
First issue Vocalion 1185; mx C-1939-B. Included through the courtesy of MCA Records.

The 1928 Jimmie Noone Apex Club group, with Earl Hines on piano, represents a distinct use and modification of the New Orleans ensemble style. Joe Poston's alto takes the lead melody, with Noone offering a highly developed, exploratory polyphonic line behind him, and Hines sometimes providing an equally effective part as well. The good-natured vocal on the somewhat salacious *Four or Five Times*, accompanied so superbly by Hines, is not untypical of the Apex Club group.

CD II

FLETCHER HENDERSON AND HIS ORCHESTRA
The Stampede
(Mus., Fletcher Henderson)
Arr., Don Redman. Rec. 5/14/26.
Fletcher Henderson (p); Russell Smith (t); Joe Smith, Rex Stewart (c); Benny Morton (tb); Buster Bailey (cl, as); Don Redman (cl, as); Coleman Hawkins (cl, ts); Charlie Dixon (bj); Ralph Escudero (tba); Kaiser Marshall (d).
Soloists: Stewart; Hawkins; Joe Smith; Henderson; Stewart.
First issue Columbia 654-D; mx 142205-3. Included through the courtesy of CBS Special Products.

For this selection, we backtrack a bit and pick up the early development of the big band.

The Stampede shows the startling effects of Armstrong's influence on an orchestra of which he had been a member. Both the cornetists, Rex Stewart (who has the opening and closing solos) and Joe Smith (who had shown a fairly mature, tart, lyric style before he heard Louis), reach out in brass hyperboles. Between their statements, there is Coleman Hawkins's tenor saxophone solo, which shows a grasp both of Armstrong's early style and of the function of his ideas as parts of a developing pattern of melody.

The arrangement by Don Redman is almost an archetype of the big band score: written passages that separate the ensemble by sections, antiphonal phrases between the sections, a written variation-on-theme (here by the clarinet trio that Redman's work made popular at the time), and solo improvisation.

Redman's structure is worth attention, too:

Introduction (Stewart)
A/A (Hawkins's solo)
Interlude
B (Smith's solo)
Interlude
C (Stewart's second solo and ensemble)

The C theme takes its first three-quarters from the A theme and the rest from B, in a musical summary-conclusion.

It is also obvious here that whereas the soloists are absorbing Armstrong's ideas of swing, the ensemble as a whole, however much power and drive it shows, does not swing. One problem certainly is the clumping rhythm section, dominated by the tuba's every-other-beat *whump*. New Orleans rhythm sections had already used a string bass on every four beats more often than they used the oompah tuba, with good reason.

FLETCHER HENDERSON AND HIS ORCHESTRA
Wrappin' It Up
(Mus., Fletcher Henderson)
Arr. Fletcher Henderson. Rec. 9/12/34.
Henry "Red" Allen, Irving Randolph, Russell Smith (t); Keg Johnson, Claude Jones (tb); Buster Bailey, Hilton Jefferson, Russell Procope (cl, as); Ben Webster (ts); Horace Henderson (p); Lawrence Lucie (g); Elmer James (b); Walter Johnson (d).
Soloists: Jefferson (as); Allen; Bailey.
First issue Decca 157; mx 38604-B. Included through the courtesy of MCA Records.

Wrappin' It Up is a fine example of Henderson's mature style, the most influential, widely imitated style of the big band era and therefore worth a detailed examination.

*Fletcher Henderson
in the 1920s. (Duncan
Schiedt Collection)*

Wrappin' It Up consists of a thirty-two measure ABAC structure which divides neatly into two sixteen-measure halves. Henderson offers an introduction and four choruses for an ensemble of twelve instrumentalists and features three soloists.

The introduction employs the first of many call-and-response patterns in the arrangement, as the brass states a kind of jazz fanfare, the saxophones respond, and a brief discourse between the two sections follows.

In the opening chorus, however, Henderson at first reverses the roles: the saxophones state the main phrases of the theme and the brasses provide a quick "Oh" or "Yeah!" between saxophone phrases. These saxophone phrases link and develop quite nicely, one to the next. For example, the second phrase modifies the last three notes of the first, the third is the same as the first, the fourth is a variant of the second, and so on.

Halfway through the opening chorus, Henderson lets the trumpets join the saxophones for a mass statement of theme, as though, by listening and responding, they had now got the idea and wanted to join in.

For his second chorus, Henderson offers his alto saxophonist Hilton Jefferson a delicate, weaving solo and backs him by a muted, chorale-like brass accompaniment—a period of relative calm.

The third chorus opens with Red Allen's fiery, agile trumpet, which is accompanied by darting saxophones and is momentarily interrupted by a comment from the whole brass section.

The climactic chorus of *Wrappin' It Up* is a strong variation on the opening, tossed back and forth between the brass players and the reed players, who have switched to clarinets. Next is a clarinet solo and then saxophone phrases, with the brass eventually joining in. The ending is a fine stroke in which one piano note cuts off the brass as they finish a deliberate, mounting cliché, which was nicely prefigured earlier in Red Allen's chorus.

Wrappin' It Up is one of several pieces that Henderson later provided for the Benny Goodman orchestra, and this version makes an interesting comparison to the one Goodman recorded in 1938. The Goodman ensemble (with a fourth saxophone, by the way) certainly plays with more precision and polish (there are a couple of obviously sloppy moments on Henderson's recording), but the general emotional tone and effect seems different. We note also in the Goodman version how indebted Harry James's trumpet solo is to Allen's original here. (Allen was a very important and influential post-Armstrong trumpeter who continued to develop.)

Henderson's music, its effect, and its influence were an important cultural contribution to American, and world, history. In one form or another, it reached and moved millions of people and helped carry the human spirit through some rather desperate times in the 1930s.

RED NICHOLS AND HIS FIVE PENNIES
Dinah

(Mus., Henry Akst; lyr., Sam M. Lewis, Joe Young)
Rec. 4/18/29.
Red Nichols, Manny Klein, Leo McConville (t)
Jack Teagarden, Bill Trone or Herb Taylor
(tb); Benny Goodman (cl); Babe Russin (ts);
Arthur Schutt (p); Carl Kress (g); Art Miller
(b); Gene Krupa (d).
Soloists: Teagarden; Goodman; Russin; Goodman; Teagarden; Goodman and Teagarden.
First issue Brunswick 4373; mx E-29709-A.
Included through the courtesy of MCA Records.

This version of *Dinah* is introduced
by Jack Teagarden, who, along with
Fletcher Henderson's Jimmy Harrison,
was one of those who set about the
business of realizing Armstrong's ideas
on trombone. Teagarden's climactic solo
here, ascending up to his thrusting
treatment of the bridge and settling into
his polyphonic comments in the brief
closing ensemble, show how well he had
done it. It remained for successor trombonists like Dickie Wells (hear *Taxi War
Dance* below) to break away to a somewhat less direct use of Armstrong.
Teagarden remained an outstanding performer, a singer as well as an instrumentalist, throughout his career.

The Red Nichols Pennies groups were
studio-assembled—the very young
Benny Goodman has a solo here—and
often gave their emphasis to forms, ensemble voicings, and chord progressions
that were experimental. But their recordings more often lacked the energy
and solo thrust that Teagarden and
Goodman give *Dinah* here.

BENNIE MOTEN'S KANSAS CITY ORCHESTRA
Moten Swing

(Mus., Bennie & Buster Moten)
Arr., Eddie Durham. Rec. 12/13/32, Camden, N.J.
Joe Keyes, Oran "Hot Lips" Page, Dee Stewart
(t); Dan Minor (tb); Eddie Durham (tb, g);
Eddie Barefield (cl, as); Jack Washington (as,
bars); Ben Webster (ts); Count Basie (p);
Leroy Berry (g); Walter Page (b); Willie
McWashington (d); Bennie Moten (dir).
Soloists: Basie; Durham (g); Barefield (as);
Page; Webster; Page.
First issue Victor 23384; mx 74847-1. Included
through the courtesy of RCA Records.

*In mid-December of 1932, in the
depths of the depression, a group of
musicians entered the RCA Victor recording studios in Camden, New Jersey, for a
marathon recording session. They were
the members of the Bennie Moten orchestra, one of the leading bands of the
Midwest....The men were demoralized,
literally hungry, and the long session
was almost the last act of this particular
manifestation of the Moten band. As
clarinet and alto soloist Eddie Barefield
has put it, "We didn't have any
money...we had to get to Camden to
record, and along comes this little guy
Archie with a raggedy old bus, and he
took us there. He got us a rabbit and
four loaves of bread, and we cooked
rabbit stew right on a pool table. That
kept us from starving, and then we went
on to make the records. Eddie Durham
was doing most of Bennie's writing then;
I made* Toby *that time. We just turned
around and made it back to Kansas City.
We hung around there for a while, not
doing much of anything...."*

*Certainly, there is nothing either in the
music or in the frequently joyous way
it's played...to indicate that the band was
in such straits at the time. Or glance at
the soon-to-be-illustrious personnel....*

*Walter Page, [by providing] a firm,
steady but exhilarating four-beats on
bass, probably had as much to do with
the character of this music as anything
else. And there is a style of music which
is fresh and rather unlike Moten's previ-*

ous music and which, in just a few years, would dominate big band jazz.

But in late 1932, apparently few people wanted to hear it. They wanted to hear earlier Moten instrumentals like Moten Stomp *(which sounds quite dated now), and they wanted to hear* South *(which Moten had first recorded in 1924, and which in its 1928 version could be heard in urban jukeboxes well into the early forties). But they didn't want to hear this music which sounds so frequently vital and undated, even now....*

Moten Swing succinctly reveals what this band achieved. Here, by late 1932, was a large jazz orchestra which could swing cleanly and precisely according to the manner of Louis Armstrong—a group which had grasped his innovative ideas of jazz rhythm and had realized and developed them in an ensemble style. Further, the piece features original melodies on a rather sophisticated chord structure borrowed from a standard popular song. Notice also how much Fats Waller there is in Basie's solo—the stride masters James P. Johnson and Luckey Roberts were Basie influences in his early days, and Waller gave Basie instruction. Notice also how personally melodious "Lips" Page is. And notice that the figures usually played...as Moten Swing *are only the final riffs in this performance.* (condensed from Martin Williams, 1965 liner notes for *Count Basie in Kansas City*, RCA 1-5180)

FATS WALLER
I Ain't Got Nobody

(Mus., Spencer Williams; lyr., Roger Graham)
Rec. 6/11/37.
Fats Waller (p).
First issue Victor 25631; mx 010656-1. Included through the courtesy of RCA Records.

Our Waller selection is not typical. It is not one of his ebullient vocal and piano burlesques of a current popular song. It is not one of his own pieces (*Honeysuckle Rose, Ain't Misbehavin'*). Nor is it one of his post-ragtime piano works (*Valentine Stomp* or *Handful of Keys*). It is not an interestingly structured blues (*Numb Fumblin'*). We pick it because it is one of his best, most

thoughtful piano performances.

Richard Hadlock says, in *Jazz Masters of the Twenties*:

*The...piano solos recorded in June 1937...are variations on standard songs—*Star Dust, Tea for Two, *Spencer Williams'* Basin Street Blues, *and* I Ain't Got Nobody, *and Fats's own* Keepin' Out of Mischief Now. *The best is* I Ain't Got Nobody *(one of Fats' favorites), which sparkles with wit (rather than comedy), musical thought, whimsicality, and real tenderness. Fats's control of dynamics throughout is exemplary.*

MEADE "LUX" LEWIS
Honky Tonk Train Blues

(Mus., Meade Lewis)
Rec. 3/7/37, Chicago.
Meade "Lux" Lewis (p).
First issue Victor 25541; mx 06301-1. Included through the courtesy of RCA Records.

Boogie woogie is a percussive blues piano style—no one knows how old—in which an ostinato bass figure, usually (but not always) played eight beats to the bar, is juxtaposed with a succession of right hand figures.

With a little coordination, the style is easy enough to play. But without the right rhythmic touch and imagination (a quite individual matter) it is very difficult to play well. In the proper hands and in small doses, it can be fascinating. One of its greatest players, Jimmy Yancey, was a rudimentary pianist by other standards. But José Iturbi, in undertaking boogie woogie, failed miserably....

The Honky Tonk Train *of Meade "Lux" Lewis is an extraordinary piece, entirely consistent and sustained, and, within its limited means, full of variety. Other pianists who have undertaken it have missed its rhythmic subtleties almost to a man and have even omitted one of its best figures...a masterpiece in a fragile genre that has all but disappeared.* (Martin Williams, *Jazz Masters in Transition, 1957-1969,* reprinted from the *New York Times,* 1969)

There was a boogie woogie craze of sorts in the late thirties and early forties when masters like Lewis, Albert Ammons, and Pete Johnson were discov-

Benny Goodman and Teddy Wilson. *(Duncan Schiedt Collection)*

ered, but public attention went mostly to amiable nonsense like *Scrub Me Mama With a Boogie Beat* and *Boogie Woogie Bugle Boy*. Early rock music borrowed boogie woogie devices and effects wholesale.

This is Lewis's third version of *Honky Tonk Train*. His first was done in 1927.

BENNY GOODMAN TRIO
Body and Soul

(Mus., Johnny Green; lyr., Robert Sauer, Ed Heyman, & Frank Eyton)
Rec. 7/13/35.
Benny Goodman (cl); Teddy Wilson (p); Gene Krupa (d).

Soloists: Goodman; Wilson; Goodman; Wilson; Goodman; Wilson; Goodman.
First issue Victor 25115; mx 92705-1. Included through the courtesy of RCA Records.

We have discussed this performance earlier in "Hearing the Melody."

Teddy Wilson's piano solo, specifically the first half of the second chorus, is a kind of miracle of originality in melody and phrasing.

There are other surviving recordings of this piece by the Goodman Trio from concerts and radio broadcasts, and a solo version from 1941 by Wilson. They make fascinating comparisons to this first one.

51

COLEMAN HAWKINS AND HIS ORCHESTRA
Body and Soul

(Mus., Johnny Green; lyr., Robert Sauer, Ed Heyman, & Frank Eyton)
Rec. 10/11/39.
Coleman Hawkins (ts); Joe Guy, Tommy Lindsay (t); Earl Hardy (tb); Jackie Fields, Eustis Moore (as); Gene Rodgers (p); William Oscar Smith (b); Arthur Herbert (d).
Soloists: Rodgers; Hawkins.
First issue Bluebird B-10253; mx 042936-1. Included through the courtesy of RCA Records.

The Goodman and Wilson treatments of *Body and Soul* are, respectively, thematic and horizontal. Coleman Hawkins's version is almost opposite to both: nonthematic (or barely thematic in its opening bars) and vertical. He has grown since his *Stampede* solo, and he has found his own style based on arpeggios (playing out the notes in a chord from bottom to top or top to bottom). His two treatments of the bridge are almost exemplary, as are the general technical-emotional contours of the performance.

Hawkins's *Body and Soul* was that rare exception, a recording that was an artistic success and influence among musicians as well as a popular hit—indeed, it was still found in American jukeboxes well into the 1950s.

COLEMAN HAWKINS QUARTET
The Man I Love

(Mus., George Gershwin; lyr., Ira Gershwin)
Rec. 12/23/43.
Coleman Hawkins (ts); Eddie Heywood (p); Oscar Pettiford (b); Shelly Manne (d).
Soloists: Heywood; Pettiford; Hawkins.
First issue Signature 9001; mx T19005. Included through the courtesy of Teresa Gramophone Co., Ltd.

The proprietor of Signature Records, Bob Thiele, was in the Coast Guard, in the "military morale" department and stationed at Manhattan Beach. A fellow member of that outfit was a young drummer who was already making a name for himself among musicians, Shelly Manne. In those days, Thiele recorded for his own pleasure and not only picked his own leaders but sometimes the sidemen as well, according to his own taste.

He remembers the Man I Love *session as happy and productive. He believes, but is not sure, that that piece was done in one take. He is sure that it was nearly destroyed when a clean-up man, carrying a wet mop, nearly walked in the studio in the middle of it. Thiele dashed out of the control room and blocked his way just in time...*

I can testify that anyone who entered a jazz nightclub in 1944 would probably hear The Man I Love *performed at this interesting tempo...It was just about the hippest thing one could do just before everybody tried to emulate Parker and Gillespie a year or so later.*

It was Hawkins's idea to do this rhythmic double-up on The Man I Love*. After Manne's introduction, Heywood...is the first soloist. And in the 1940s Heywood obviously was a jazz pianist (and not yet the author of such ditties as* Canadian Sunset*)...We also hear on this piece from Oscar Pettiford, then one of the most promising bassists in jazz (and a couple of years later, after he came to terms with bebop, one of the most fulfilled bassists in jazz).*

Then, Hawkins. It is impossible truly to account for the excellence of Hawkins's solo on The Man I Love *since it is impossible to explain excellence. But one can point out some of the things that contribute to it. There is Hawkins's tenor sound of this period, less hard and brittle than his sound in the thirties, and more appropriate, I think, to his manifestly expanding musical sophistication. The second is his rhythmic variety. At medium and fast tempos, Hawkins's phrasing usually sets up the expectation of a driving, regular accentuation: HEAVY beat, light beat/HEAVY, light/ HEAVY, light/HEAVY, light/etc. The ingenuity comes when he breaks up that expectation with rhythmic surprises, as he does so well here. Then there is the variety in his melodic ideas here, as traditional sounding riffs and blues phrases interplay with his more showy arpeggios.* (Condensed from Martin Williams, liner notes to the 1963 reissue *Classic Tenors*, Contact LP CM 3)

Billie Holiday. (Photo by Charles Stewart)

BILLIE HOLIDAY AND HER ORCHESTRA
He's Funny That Way
(Mus. & lyr., Robert Whiting & Neil Moret)
Rec. 9/13/37.
Billie Holiday (voc); Buck Clayton (t); Buster Bailey (cl); Lester Young (ts); Claude Thornhill (p); Freddy Green (g); Walter Page (b); Jo Jones (d).
Soloists: Young; Holiday and Young; Clayton; Holiday and Young.
First issue Vocalion/Okeh 3748; mx 21689-1. Included through the courtesy of CBS Special Products.

Billie Holiday once said that she grew up loving Bessie Smith's power and Louis Armstrong's style.

It is surely a tribute to the resources of both artists that the stark, near-tragic (though sometimes ironically joyous) work of Billie Holiday could have been so strongly influenced by the life-affirming music of Louis Armstrong. But one should remember that it was also the more emotionally complex trumpet work of Armstrong that inspired her as well as his vocal style.

He's Funny That Way is beautifully, consistently acted; melody, mood, emotion, voice quality are a unity. Her joyous but salty rise at the final "But why should I leave him..." is one of those superb touches that only Holiday's rare, intuitive musical taste could account for.

The performance is further enriched by the sublime improvised counterpoint of Lester Young. "In Lester Young, she found rapport but emotional and stylistic contrast, and two eras of jazz met in sometimes transporting discourse." (Martin Williams, *The Jazz Tradition*)

BILLIE HOLIDAY AND HER ORCHESTRA
These Foolish Things
(Mus., Jack Strachey & Harry Link; lyr., Holt Marvell)
Rec. 3/26/52, Los Angeles.
Billie Holiday (voc); Oscar Peterson (p); Barney Kessel (g); Ray Brown (b); Alvin Stoller (d).
First issue Clef 89002; mx 769-3. Included through the courtesy of PolyGram Records.

Billie Holiday recorded *These Foolish Things* twice. In her earlier version (the vocal chorus in the middle of a 1938 Teddy Wilson recording), she rides through the harmonic structure of the piece in effective, if musically unsubtle, ways. The reading here is superior in almost every way, and although Holiday's vocal instrument had deteriorated, her musicianship had grown greatly. She is very well aware of the harmonic structure of the piece, and she virtually re-writes the song's A section into a deceptively complex melody of her own:

Holiday is aided throughout by Oscar Peterson, from his contrastingly conceived introduction onward, and the whole performance has a sustained, almost overpowering aura.

Original melody

Billie Holiday's version

RECORD SIDE 5

ELLA FITZGERALD
You'd Be So Nice to Come Home To
(Mus. & lyr., Cole Porter)
Rec. in stereo 7/64, Antibes, France.
Ella Fitzgerald (voc); Roy Eldridge (t); Tommy Flanagan (p); Bill Yancey (b); Gus Johnson (d).
First issue Verve V6-4065; mx unknown. Included through the courtesy of PolyGram Records.

Ella Fitzgerald, as you may know, is a singer's singer. Her control is sure, her notes are clear, her pitch is precise. Her range isn't wide, but her voice has body, perhaps as much body as a popular singer is entitled to. Her rhythm is im-peccable. And she swings, still in the manner of her beginning, circa 1936. But for all her professional control she can improvise, and her final chorus or so may give impressions of a gleeful abandon.

Ella Fitzgerald is also the public's singer. She packs them in at the record shops, auditoriums, and night clubs. But she is not, as you may not know, a reviewer's singer—at least not in some quarters....

No, Ella Fitzgerald is not capable of tragedy. She is capable of good melodrama...and of a kind of nostalgic pensiveness....To her detractors, all the rest is engaging shallowness. But for me,

Ella Fitzgerald. *(Photo by Charles Stewart)*

hers is the stuff of joy, a joy that is profound and ever replenished—perhaps
from the self-discovery that, for all her
equipment as a singer's singer, she is
absolutely incapable of holding anything
back. (Martin Williams, Jazz Heritage)

Fitzgerald's heritage is interesting: it
goes back to Ethel Waters but also
comes directly from the white singer
Connee Boswell.

The totally compelling You'd Be So
Nice to Come Home To is treated with
more improvisational freedom than
most of Ella Fitzgerald's studio-made
recordings. But as a location recording,
done at an open-air jazz festival in
France, it does not capture her unique,
clear voice quality so well.

Among her pre-1961 studio recordings, the general level is very, very high,
and from among her "song book" series,
the Harold Arlen album can be particularly recommended.

ART TATUM
Willow Weep for Me
(Mus. & lyr., Ann Ronell)
Rec. 7/13/49, Los Angeles
Art Tatum (p).
First issue Capitol 15520; mx 5039. Included
through the courtesy of Capitol Records.

Too Marvelous for Words
(Mus., Richard Whiting; lyr. Johnny Mercer)
Rec. 7/3/55, Beverly Hills.
Art Tatum (p).
First issue 20th Century Fox SFX 3029. In-
cluded through the courtesy of PolyGram
Records.

Tatum's keyboard virtuosity is obvious. Less obvious to the newcomer perhaps are the subtleties of his touch, the
richness of his harmonic imagination,
and the ultimate artistry with which he
uses each of his resources.

*For Art Tatum, performing carried
specific responsibilities, some of which
reflected the traditions of the European
concert hall. To accomplish his goals, he
needed musical constants or signposts;
standard popular songs, with their balanced melodies, harmonies, and phrase
lengths, provided them. In addition, he
crafted basic outlines or arrangements*

*for each of the pieces in his repertory.
Mastery and control of his materials
were essential to him. To rely heavily on
intuition was a luxury reserved for informal occasions.*

*For him, the challenge of improvisa-
tion was a challenge of re-composition,
and it was his self-imposed limitations
that produced his amazing, suspenseful
flights.*

*Tatum was a musical juggler and a
master of suspense. He relished battling
the barline. Many of his seemingly out-
of-tempo trips are produced by a masterful kind of rubato [delay] and are
really in tempo. He devised an array of
decorative embellishments that seemed
to appear in almost every performance
but never in the same order and never
out of context.*

*Tatum was not a spinner of long me-
lodic lines like Teddy Wilson or Coleman
Hawkins, who often replaced a written
melody with one completely their own.*

Willow Weep for Me, *with its blues-
like character, is a 32-bar AABA piece,
with a bridge in minor. Tatum's performance shows his ability to combine
his European-derived virtuosity with his
very Afro-American blues feeling.*

*Only two choruses long, the perform-
ance is a marvel of construction and
content. It begins with a typical four-bar
introductory vamp-til-ready that serves
as a "glue" for the sections that follow.
The first six bars of the A theme in its
first two appearances are stated ad lib,
but with Tatum, ad lib statements have a
rhythmic momentum all their own and
are good lessons in how to "breathe"
and sing a melody out-of-tempo. The
last two bars of each A section recall the
vamp from the introduction.*

*Going into the first bridge, Tatum slips
into that perfect, walking blues tempo
that is so elusive. And notice his variations, how the left hand double-time run
doesn't break the rhythmic flow but actually gives it push.*

*The last eight bars of this chorus re-
semble the first eight, and contain many
of the same incredible substitute harmonies, this time in tempo. The same two-*

Art Tatum in the late 1940s. *(Duncan Schiedt Collection)*

bar vamp from the intro then sets up the second chorus.

Tatum begins that second chorus by departing from the melody to create a pure, from-the-gut blues statement, complete with "vocal" effects achieved through an uncanny ability to "crush" notes and whole chords on the piano in a way that simulates the slur and growl effects of singers and horn players. Bars 9–12 of this chorus, by the way, are a variation of bars 1–4.

Notice also the "outside," twelve-tone effects early in the second chorus. When Tatum did take off, he utilized both the chord changes and his unsurpassed control of meter. (In this he was obviously influenced by Earl Hines, another rhythmic virtuoso.) Typically, such non-thematic Tatum fragments are not lyric; they are abstract, intense, almost anti-melodic, and sometimes difficult to follow.

The bridge in the second chorus is a more elaborate version of the one in the first; again, it relies heavily on the melody, but with a compendium of arpeggios, runs, and harmonic substitutions that may tend to overwhelm laymen and fascinate (but traumatize) musicians. The last eight bars and coda of the second chorus are played accelerando–ad lib. And that coda, again based on the vamp from the intro, is developed into a kind of miniature piece.

Too Marvelous for Words is a thirty-two bar AABA piece that appeals to musicians mainly because of its harmonic structure. The bridge modulates (moves in and out of its key) in a unique way and is tricky to negotiate smoothly. The last A section has a clever tag. The piece is a difficult one to improvise on.

In this performance we have the "after hours" Tatum, stretching out, more adventurous in an informal setting—an example of musical daring and tightrope walking.

The performance starts with a fade-in, and there are three and one-half choruses; that is, after the third chorus Tatum returns to the bridge and finishes a half-chorus.

The complexity of his improvisation here precludes detailed analysis, so I will just point out a few highlights.

Tatum embarks on a harmonic flight that breaks at the very limits of the key center (G major). To these ears, it sounds as though he states the first part of a sequential phrase and then completes it a half step higher or lower, as the case may be. However, these transitions (they aren't long enough to be termed modulations) are done with substitute, altered chord changes that create an effect of suspended animation or musical weightlessness.

There are other delights. Notice the last eight bars of the first chorus. Here Tatum is concerned with toying with the meter. His rhythmic shifts are extremely hard to follow, even for a trained ear. But close listening shows that he is always on the mark and in complete control.

Indeed, the whole performance is remarkable, and its musical implications are those of a giant talent whose artistry will be felt as long as making music is a human pursuit. (Dick Katz)

JIMMIE LUNCEFORD AND HIS ORCHESTRA
Organ Grinder's Swing

(Mus., Will Hudson; lyr., Mitchell Parish & Irving Mills)
Arr., Sy Oliver. Rec. 8/31/36.
Sy Oliver, Eddie Tompkins, Paul Webster (t); Russell Bowles, Elmer Crumbley, Eddie Durham (tb); Willie Smith, Earl Carruthers (cl, as, bars); Dan Grissom (cl, as); Joe Thomas (cl, ts); Laforet Dent (as); Edwin Wilcox (p, cel); Al Norris (g); Moses Allen (b); Jimmy Crawford (d); Jimmie Lunceford (dir).
Soloists: Oliver and Carruthers (bars); Wilcox (cel); Norris; Smith (cl); Webster; Oliver; Oliver and Carruthers (bars).
First issue Decca 908; mx 61246-A. Included through the courtesy of MCA Records.

Sy Oliver's classic miniature for the Lunceford band, based on a children's teasing jingle, was catchy and appealing and became an international hit. It also showed that Lunceford's was the one band aside from Ellington's that broke away early from the Henderson antiphonal (call-and-response) style.

As usual, Oliver used a variety of phrases and ideas most effectively. But the performance also depends on the typical discipline and precision of the Lunceford orchestra. Oliver uses dynamic, sonorous, and timbral contrasts uniquely, from his haunting Ellingtonesque opening (muted trumpet, trombone, clarinet) through the assertive baritone sax, the growl trumpet (Oliver), the celeste, the temple block, the bluesy guitar, and the almost pianissimo saxes—all perfectly contained by *Organ Grinder's Swing*'s careful introduction and coda.

CASSETTE SIDE D

GENE KRUPA AND HIS ORCHESTRA
Rockin' Chair
(Mus., Hoagy Carmichael)
Arr., Benny Carter. Rec. 7/2/41.
Roy Eldridge, Graham Young, Torg Halten, Norman Murphy (t); Babe Wagner, Jay Kelliher, John Grassi (tb); Mascagni Ruffo, Sam Listengart (as); Sam Musiker (cl, ts); Walter Bates (ts); Milton Raskin (p); Ray Biondi (g); Ed Mihelich (b); Gene Krupa (d).
Soloists: Eldridge; Musiker (cl); Eldridge.
First issue Okeh 6352; mx 30830-1. Included through the courtesy of CBS Special Products.

Like Hawkins's *Body and Soul,* this ballad interpretation by Roy Eldridge was an unexpected success and a kind of instant classic. Eldridge was the most original trumpet soloist between Armstrong and Gillespie and the most powerful. Armstrong's *I Gotta Right to Sing the Blues,* Eldridge's *Rockin' Chair,* and Gillespie's *I Can't Get Started* make a kind of continuity of jazz trumpet ballads.

Eldridge once said that he had thought he was a good trumpet soloist but when he really heard Louis Armstrong, Eldridge realized he hadn't been "telling a story." *Rockin' Chair,* with its partly tongue-in-cheek ending, tells its own story.

THE CHOCOLATE DANDIES, FEATURING ROY ELDRIDGE AND BENNY CARTER
I Can't Believe That You're in Love with Me [excerpt]
(Mus., Jimmy McHugh; lyr., Clarence Gaskill) Rec. 5/25/40.
Roy Eldridge (t); Benny Carter (as); Coleman Hawkins (ts); Bernard Addison (g); John Kirby (b); Sidney Catlett (d).
Soloists: Eldridge; Carter.
First issue Commodore 1506; mx R-2997-1.
Included through the courtesy of Commodore Records.

I have abridged this performance so that it begins directly on Eldridge's searing, inventive solo, with no previous statement of the McHugh melody, which shows up in a paraphrased counterpoint at the end of the performance.

Benny Carter's alto solo is a minor gem. At the time, many a saxophonist would have been running up and down the chord changes with as much of Coleman Hawkins's manner as they could grasp (and possibly none of his art). But Carter's treatment spreads out fragments and ideas in long meter over the chord progression. Notice also the help he gets from Sidney Catlett, one of the great drummers.

In this session, originally recorded on the label of a small New York record shop that specialized in jazz, the ensemble was called the Chocolate Dandies. This often-used recording pseudonym (which may now seem in questionable taste) goes back to 1928 and was most often used, as here, for Fletcher Henderson sidemen working on their own.

LIONEL HAMPTON AND HIS ORCHESTRA
When Lights Are Low
(Mus., Benny Carter; lyr., Spencer Williams) Arr., Benny Carter. Rec. 9/11/39.
Dizzy Gillespie (t); Benny Carter (as); Coleman Hawkins, Ben Webster, Chu Berry (ts); Clyde Hart (p); Charlie Christian (g); Milt Hinton (b); Cozy Cole (d); Lionel Hampton (vib).
Soloists: Hampton; Carter; Hampton; Hawkins; Hart.
First issue Victor 26371; mx 041406-1. Included through the courtesy of RCA Records.

The vibraharp (or vibraphone) was explored and developed largely by jazz musicians, and Lionel Hampton was the first jazz vibraharpist. His swing is as impeccable as Ella Fitzgerald's, his harmonic sense is sure (and has grown over the years), and his basic orientation is that of a former drummer.

While still a member of the Benny Goodman Quartet and Sextet (for which he contributed excellent solos on, for example, *Sweet Sue* and *Gone with "What" Wind*) Hampton made a series of records on his own with pickup personnel, usually from the Basie, Henderson, Goodman, Cab Calloway, Hines, or Ellington bands. Some of the records were highly informal; others were more formal, like this one composed, arranged, and directed by Benny Carter, whose ably sophisticated writing style was built on Redman's and Henderson's. Carter was (along with Johnny Hodges) one of the great alto saxophonists before Charlie Parker's arrival.

André Hodeir, in *Jazz: Its Evolution and Essence,* speaks of Carter's "delicately inventive" solo here, and says that if he, Hampton, and Hawkins never played better, it is largely because they were helped by an impeccable rhythm section. "Any musician who has ever played in a jazz band knows the stimulation that can be expected from a harmony that falls just right or a way of playing cymbals that really swings."

Hodeir goes on to describe the rhythmic basis of *When Lights Are Low:*

First of all, there is the incomparable homogeneity of the accompaniment— Clyde Hart (piano), Charlie Christian (guitar), Milton Hinton (bass), and Cozy Cole (drums). It doesn't seem that there are four instruments played by four musicians; the impression of unity is so strong that the plurality of voices becomes questionable. Even the dry slap of the high-hat cymbal on the even-numbered beats—a holdover—is not really heard. By fitting in together so perfectly, the timbres become fuller and richer by mutual contact. Such a blending would not have been possible ten years or even five years earlier, when

the training of accompanists still had ground to cover. It was not for nothing that two generations of specialists in rhythm had worn down their fingers looking, whether they fully realized it or not, for a way to express the swing they felt in themselves. The young men benefited from the effort of their seniors. Isn't that just what every real tradition makes possible?

And the one flaw:

It is hardly surprising that big bands are much more rarely satisfying than small ones in swing. Playing in a section, very good musicians occasionally get the notes in the wrong place, either because they have misinterpreted what the arranger wanted or because they have misunderstood what their section leader wanted. Errors of this kind can be partially redeemed by the other musicians if their part is more prominent. Still, the swing invariably suffers. The example of the final ensemble in When Lights Are Low *is significant in this respect; every rhythmic weakness, however small, results in a proportional weakness in the swing.*

QUINTETTE OF THE HOT CLUB OF FRANCE
Dinah
(Mus., Henry Akst; lyr., Sam M. Lewis, Joe Young)
Rec. 12/34, Paris.
Stephane Grappelli (vn); Django Reinhardt, Roger Chaput, Joseph Reinhardt (g); Louis Vola (b).
Soloists: D. Reinhardt; Grappelli.
First issue Ultraphone AP-1422; mx P-77161.
Included through the courtesy of Vogue Productions Internationales Phonographiques.

We already know from the work of Lonnie Johnson on *Hotter Than That* that an effective solo jazz guitar was around in the 1920s. Another outstanding guitarist appeared in the 1930s, as did the first really important jazzman who was not an American, both in the person of a Belgian-born gypsy musician, Django Reinhardt. What is more, Django's early companion Stephane Grappelli was a violinist with true improvisational talent on an instrument that is notoriously difficult to make swing. Their gifts are well demonstrated here in their two choruses apiece on *Dinah*, from the very first recording date of the quintet they co-led.

Reinhardt begins with an invention and introduces a fragment of the melody only on his second phrase. His well-paced solo shows how soundly he had learned the lessons of some of the great jazz players, but he is unmistakably a Belgian gypsy guitarist as well. And behind Grappelli, at points he even evokes a whole band.

COUNT BASIE AND HIS ORCHESTRA
Doggin' Around
(Mus., Herschel Evans & Edgar W. Battle)
Arr., Herschel Evans & Edgar W. Battle. Rec. 6/6/38.
Count Basie (p); Buck Clayton, Harry Edison, Ed Lewis (t); Eddie Durham, Dan Minor, Benny Morton (tb); Earle Warren (as); Jack Washington (as, bars); Herschel Evans, Lester Young (ts); Freddie Green (g); Walter Page (b); Jo Jones (d).
Soloists: Basie; Warren; Evans; Edison; Washington; Basie; Young.
First issue Decca 1965; mx 63920-A. Included through the courtesy of MCA Records.

RECORD SIDE 6

Taxi War Dance
(Mus., Count Basie, Lester Young)
Arr., Buck Clayton. Rec. 3/19/39.
Buck Clayton, Shad Collins, Harry Edison, Ed Lewis (t); Dan Minor, Benny Morton, Dickie Wells (tb); Earle Warren, Jack Washington (as); Buddy Tate, Lester Young (ts); Count Basie (p); Freddie Green (g); Walter Page (b); Jo Jones (d).

Soloists: Basie; Young; Wells; Young; Basie; Young; Basie; Young; Basie; Young; Page; Jones.
First issue Vocalion 4748; mx 24242-1. Included through the courtesy of CBS Special Products.

COUNT BASIE'S KANSAS CITY SEVEN
Lester Leaps In
(Mus., Lester Young)
Rec. 9/5/39.
Count Basie (p); Buck Clayton (t); Dickie Wells (tb); Lester Young (ts); Freddie Green (g); Walter Page (b); Jo Jones (d).
Soloists: Basie; Young; Basie; Young; Basie; Young; Basie; Young; Basie; Young; Basie.
First issue Vocalion 5118; mx 25297-1. Included through the courtesy of CBS Special Products.

Basie could stride skillfully and joyously....But when he dropped the oom-pah *of stride bass, Basie's right hand accents were no longer heavy or light but all equal, and with Page taking care of the basic beats, the pianist's rather limited melodic vocabulary was suddenly released. Basie could form solo after solo out of a handful of phrases that quickly became familiar but were always somehow fresh because they were always struck, shaded, enunciated and pronounced differently; he discovered the superbly individual piano touch which defies imitation, and which can cause subtle percussive and accentual nuances in the most apparently repetitive ideas.*

Similarly he shifted the very function of jazz ensemble piano. He no longer accompanied in the old way; he commented, encouraged, propelled, and interplayed....

His solo on Doggin' Around *is a classic of linking and occasionally contrasting melodic ideas, and is probably his masterpiece....*

Lester Young created a new aesthetic, not only for the tenor saxophone but for all jazz. One compares him usually with Coleman Hawkins, and the comparison is handy and instructive, but one might compare him with everyone who had preceded him....

There seems to me no question that...Young was the most gifted and original improviser between Louis Armstrong and Charlie Parker. He simply defied the rules and made new ones by example. His sound was light, almost vibratoless. He showed that such a sound could command a whole orchestra by understatement. His style de-

The great Count Basie Orchestra. Seated, right, with his chair and saxophone typically at an angle, is Lester Young.
(Duncan Schiedt Collection)

pended on an original and flexible use of the even, four beats which Armstrong's work made the norm. The beats were not inflexibly heavy or light in Young—indeed an occasional accent might even fall a shade ahead of the beat or behind it. And he did not phrase four measures at a time....

Young's solo on Count Basie's Doggin' Around *is a handy example, and one of the best. He begins, actually, by phrasing under the final two bars of Basie's piano chorus (thus does "Lester leap in"). His own chorus starts with a single note in a full bar of music....His second musical phrase begins at the second bar and dances gracefully through the seventh, unbroken. His eighth bar is silent— balancing the opening perhaps. In nine he begins his third phrase, which links logically with his second. But the basic impulse here is not breaking through the four and eight-bar phrases, nor in the daring symmetry of balancing one casual note at the beginning against a silence eight bars later. It is in his accents, in a sort of freely dancing, rhythmic impulse, which seems almost to dictate*

how his melodies shall move.

Harmonically, what Lester Young did *was show how original one could be with the materials already at hand. By means of a marvelous ear, and a refusal to allow a literal reading of chords to detain him, he might freely, casually, and tantalizingly phrase several beats ahead of a coming chord change and let its arrival show how right he was all along. Similarly, he might phrase behind an already departed chord, and let the arrival of his melody notes tell us that he knew it had been there after all. His opening chorus on* Taxi War Dance *contains a bold enough use of such horizontal, linear phrases to have captivated a whole generation of players, and to seem bold still.*

Thus one might say that his originality was not harmonic, but a-harmonic. In general what he did was hit the tonic chord, and read through the others as his ear and sense of melody dictated. (Martin Williams, *The Jazz Tradition*)

Also notice the bridge of Lester Young's *Doggin' Around* solo: a series of apparently disconnected spurts are tied together by a single four-bar phrase at the end.

Like all of the giants, Lester possesses a tremendous beat. He is one of those rare musicians who can swing an entire band. The massive swing of the Basie orchestra became even more exciting when Lester soloed...He is the most relaxed of musicians. His notes flowed like water out of a tap and the source showed no signs of depletion.

Lester's detachment was unshakable. He always seemed to be in a world of his own. Heard in person, in the midst of the happy jungle of Basie's orchestral sound, or on record, Lester gave the impression of impassioned absorption. On records his solos glow with a radiance like the light from another planet. In the parlance of the times, he was "out of this world."

The Lester Young style is essentially romantic. It is uninhibited and relaxed, sensitive, imaginative, deeply subjective. It is the very intimate communication of an artist who was voicing the ideas of the day in the language of the next decade.

Lester was always spontaneous. Less disciplined than Hawkins, he is nonetheless a musician whose product is orderly and structural. But these qualities— balance and unity of parts, clarity of concept—lie beneath the surface, under the luminous texture of notes. (Ross Russell, "Bebop," in *The Art of Jazz*)

Lester Leaps In is a classic performance by Young and Basie with a more than able contribution by Clayton. The inspirational interplay of Basie's piano accompaniment is almost the equal of Young's inventive brilliance.

Early Basie recordings with classic Lester Young solos have been reissued in a series of albums. There is small group music with Young also on the Commodore label, which can be particularly recommended for one session on which Young played clarinet as well as tenor. From a somewhat later period, there is the superb *These Foolish Things,* last available on the Blue Note label.

BENNY GOODMAN SEXTET FEATURING CHARLIE CHRISTIAN AND COUNT BASIE
I Found a New Baby
(Mus., Jack Palmer, Spencer Williams)
Rec. 1/15/41.
Benny Goodman (cl); Cootie Williams (t); George Auld (ts); Count Basie (p); Charlie Christian (elec g); Artie Bernstein (b); Jo Jones (d).
Soloists: Goodman; Christian; Basie; Williams; Auld; Jones.
First issue Columbia 36039; mx CO-29514-1. Included through the courtesy of CBS Special Products.

Charlie Christian was not the first jazz guitar soloist; we have already heard from Lonnie Johnson and Django Reinhardt. But Christian, playing amplified guitar in a style based on a saxophone style—closest probably to Lester Young's—was a rare jazzman by any standard, aside from considerations of instrument.

He had a scant two years of public exposure, chiefly as a member of Goodman's small ensembles, and was dead at twenty-five. His work has been a major influence on virtually all subsequent jazz guitarists (and there have been many outstanding ones since him).

This version of *I Found a New Baby* contains a classic Christian solo, a superb improvised, self-contained instrumental melody, frequently used as a warm-up and exercise piece by guitarists for decades after.

BENNY GOODMAN SEXTET FEATURING CHARLIE CHRISTIAN
Breakfast Feud [composite]
(Mus., Benny Goodman)
Rec. 1/15/41 (Solos 1-4) and 12/19/40 (5).
Solos 1-4: Benny Goodman (cl); Charlie Christian (elec g); Cootie Williams (t); George Auld (ts); Count Basie (p); Artie Bernstein (b); Jo Jones (d).
Solo 5: substitute Ken Kersey (p); Harry Jaeger (d).
First issue: Solos 1-3, Columbia CL 652; mx 29512-?; solo 4, Columbia 36039; mx 29512-2; solo 5, Columbia G 30779; mx 29259-?. Included through the courtesy of CBS Special Products.

This remarkable composite tape comes from two recording dates. Each Christian solo is introduced by a four-bar ensemble passage, after which he completes that chorus and then plays another. Despite some differences in tempo, the solos make up remarkable evidence of Christian's inventiveness and his imaginative blues work.

A singular aspect of his phrasing is the unusual length of his melodic lines, consisting of even and cleanly executed eighth notes. His meter was delineated by the subtle accent of certain of these eighth notes. There are several varied examples of this technique on Breakfast Feud, *which was spliced together from... previously unissued takes. These solos are individual and original, the phrasing and accents within each one being unpredictable. In the initial three-bar phrase in the first of these solos, Christian shifts the metric accent from the normally strong first beat to the secondary third beat, thereby creating the illusion that he is starting his phrase on a pick-up from the previous chorus, when in reality he is starting on the first beat of the chorus. He molded the contour of this phrase so that the melodic peaks also occur on the accented third beats. This type of practice, unusual to jazz musicians at the time, reveals another facet of Christian's rhythmic daring and resourcefulness. In his other...* Breakfast Feud *solos his phrases fall into entirely different patterns. These...solos provide rich ground for analysis in that they demonstrate, independently one to the other (but here placed in series), the Christian techniques in dealing with basically the same blues derivatives.* (Aram Avakian and Bob Prince, liner notes to *Charlie Christian with the Benny Goodman Sextet,* Columbia CL 652.)

CD III

DUKE ELLINGTON AND HIS ORCHESTRA
East St. Louis Toddle-Oo
(Mus., Bubber Miley, Duke Ellington)
Arr., Duke Ellington. Rec. 12/19/27.

Duke Ellington (p); Bubber Miley, Louis Metcalf (t); Joe Nanton (tb); Otto Hardwicke (ss, as, bars); Harry Carney (cl, as, bars); Rudy Jackson (cl, ts); Fred Guy (bj); Wellman Braud (b); Sonny Greer (d).
Soloists: Miley; Carney (bars); Nanton; Jackson (cl); Miley.
First issue Victor 21703; mx 41245-2. Included through the courtesy of RCA Records.

DUKE ELLINGTON AND HIS FAMOUS ORCHESTRA
The New East St. Louis Toodle-O
(Mus., Bubber Miley, Duke Ellington)
Arr., Duke Ellington. Rec. 3/5/37.
Duke Ellington (p); Wallace Jones, Cootie Williams (t); Rex Stewart (c); Joe Nanton, Lawrence Brown (tb); Juan Tizol (vtb); Barney Bigard (cl, ts); Johnny Hodges (cl, as, ts); Harry Carney (cl, bars); Otto Hardwicke (as); Fred Guy (g); Hayes Alvis, Billy Taylor (b); Sonny Greer (d); Freddie Jenkins (chimes).
Soloists: Williams; Bigard (cl); Williams.
First issue Master 101; mx M-180-1. Included through the courtesy of CBS Special Products.

The juxtaposition of these two versions—made ten years apart—of one of Ellington's earliest important pieces not only attests to his growth but beautifully reveals the nature and subtlety of that growth.

Like several of his early pieces, *East St. Louis* was a collaboration between the leader and his star, King Oliver–influenced trumpeter Bubber Miley. The original title word was not *Toddle-Oo* but Toad-low; and referred, as Ellington once explained, to an old man of East St. Louis, so bent with age that he walked as low as a toad.

The earlier version consists of an AABA song-form section and a secondary theme (C):
Introduction
  A (Miley)
  A (Miley)
  B (Miley)
  A (Miley)
  C (actually a variation on C—Harry Carney)
  C (variation—Joe Nanton)
  A (Rudy Jackson on clarinet)

AA (Jackson)

C (the first full statement of the theme; the brass dominates.)

A (Miley)

Miley's forcefulness dominates the performance to the point of imbalance. Ellington's contribution is small and perhaps a bit chic. The secondary strain (rather close to *I Wish I Could Shimmy Like My Sister Kate* and other themes going back well into ragtime) seems inappropriate. Perhaps Ellington also found it inappropriate: in the several records he made of *East St. Louis* in the 1920s, the C theme was shifted around to various places in the arrangement. Here it appears twice in variation before it appears fully.

In the 1937 version, *New East St. Louis*, the C theme is gone, and we have two choruses of AABA. The performance is a fine example of the true collaboration of the composer and his musicians. Cootie Williams exhibits the subtle, personal development of the plunger-muted trumpet style, and it is beautifully balanced by Ellington's varied setting, particularly in the climactic, closing version of the A theme. Notice also the keenly played plunger responses by the full trumpet section during the first bridge, and Barney Bigard's liquid clarinet responses to the trombone-dominated variations in the second chorus, followed by his domination of the bridge.

Then there is the growth of the orchestra itself, its swing, and the obvious improvements of its rhythm section.

DUKE ELLINGTON AND HIS FAMOUS ORCHESTRA
Diminuendo in Blue
Crescendo in Blue

(Mus., Duke Ellington)
Arr., Duke Ellington. Rec. 9/20/37.
Duke Ellington (p); Wallace Jones, Cootie Williams (t); Rex Stewart (c); Joe Nanton, Lawrence Brown (tb); Barney Bigard (cl); Johnny Hodges (cl, ss, as); Harry Carney (cl, as, bars); Otto Hardwicke (as, bsx); Fred Guy (g); Billy Taylor (b); Sonny Greer (d).
Soloist: Ellington.
First issue Brunswick 8004; mx M-648-1-2 & M-649-1-2. Included through the courtesy of CBS Special Products.

This performance, originally issued on two sides of a 78-rpm disc, had an interesting history in the Ellington repertory. It followed *Creole Rhapsody* (1931) and the remarkable *Reminiscing in Tempo* (1935) as one of Ellington's several early efforts at breaking through the time limits of the recording process and at composing an extended work. In the 1940s, however, he sometimes performed the *Diminuendo* separately or spliced it to his *Transblucency* (1946), which was based in part on *Blue Light* from 1938. Then in 1956 Ellington revived *Diminuendo and Crescendo in Blue,* with an extended middle solo by tenor saxophonist Paul Gonsalves, to great success.

This piece remains a fascinating Ellington treatment of the blues, notable for its exceptionally well paced variety of orchestral textures and its typically personal individual manipulation of rhythms and accents of the past, from the Charleston period forward into the swing era. *Diminuendo* plays flexibly with the blues form, expanding the twelve-measure chorus to fourteen and using some subdivisions of two and a half bars while moving its tonality from B-flat through G, C, A-flat, D-flat, and E-flat in a singular if imperfectly executed performance.

DUKE ELLINGTON AND HIS FAMOUS ORCHESTRA
Ko-Ko

(Mus., Duke Ellington)
Arr., Duke Ellington. Rec. 3/6/40, Chicago.
Duke Ellington (p); Wallace Jones, Cootie Williams (t); Rex Stewart (c); Joe Nanton, Lawrence Brown (tb); Juan Tizol (vtb); Barney Bigard (cl, ts); Otto Hardwicke, Johnny Hodges (as); Ben Webster (ts); Harry Carney (bars); Fred Guy (g); Jimmy Blanton (b); Sonny Greer (d).
Soloists: Tizol; Nanton; Ellington; Blanton.
First issue Victor 26577; mx 044889-2. Included through the courtesy of RCA Records.

Ko-Ko is a twelve-bar blues in the minor and, in this version, perhaps the single most celebrated instrumental per-

The Ellington touch at the Randall's Island Jazz Festival, 1938.
(Duncan Schiedt Collection)

formance in Ellington's entire recorded work. It was originally dedicated to the drum ceremonies that centered in Congo Square in pre–Civil War New Orleans, survivals of African worship. And one might say that the entire piece develops out of the tom-tom pattern in its introduction. The opening melody is simple (although it is decidedly instrumental, not vocal, in quality), but the harmonic and melodic material is quite sophisticated. The opening exposition is carried antiphonally by valve trombonist Juan Tizol and the ensemble back and forth. For the next two choruses another trombonist, Joe Nanton, takes over for a solo, and his simple, colorful, earthy style and manipulation of his plunger mute over the bell of his horn make his a different instrument.

Nanton is accompanied predominantly by muted brass. Following Nanton's two choruses, Ellington uses a simplification of the same brass figure, continuing under his own piano solo. His music is full of such imaginative patterns of likeness and contrast.

Ko-Ko is evidence also of the importance of bassist Jimmy Blanton to the Ellington orchestra and, with his strong attention to the proper note of the proper chord in the proper place, to the future role of his instrument in jazz.

RECORD SIDE 7

CASSETTE SIDE E

DUKE ELLINGTON AND HIS FAMOUS ORCHESTRA
Concerto for Cootie
(Mus., Duke Ellington)
Arr., Duke Ellington. Rec. 3/15/40, Chicago.
Duke Ellington (p); Wallace Jones, Cootie Williams (t); Rex Stewart (c); Joe Nanton, Lawrence Brown (tb); Juan Tizol (vtb); Barney Bigard (cl, ts); Otto Hardwicke, Johnny Hodges (as); Ben Webster (ts); Harry Carney (bars); Fred Guy (g); Jimmy Blanton (b); Sonny Greer (d).
Soloist: Williams.
First issue Victor 26598; mx 049016-1. Included through the courtesy of RCA Records.

The opening theme of *Concerto for Cootie* was later rewritten in a simplified form as the song *Do Nothing Til You Hear from Me.* In its original version, it is, in contrast to *Ko-Ko*, harmonically simple but aurally rich.

It is dedicated to the variety of sounds that Williams resourcefully evokes from his open horn and from the use of several mutes in several ways: manipulated plunger on open horn, plunger over the small "pixie" version of the straight-mute, plunger in tight, and so on.

The opening section is in AABA form, but the A strain is ten measures instead of the usual eight, and each statement of A involves a variation in melody and texture, from both soloist and his accompaniment. Thus the performance becomes AA^1BA^2. A transition then changes the key, and Williams states the beautiful, expansive, and subsequently neglected C theme on open horn. Following that, there is a return to a truncated (six-bar) variation on A, and a rich, imaginatively extended coda of ten bars.

DUKE ELLINGTON AND HIS FAMOUS ORCHESTRA
Cotton Tail
(Mus., Duke Ellington)
Rec. 5/4/40, Hollywood.
Personnel as above.
Soloists: Williams; Webster, Carney; Ellington.
First issue Victor 26610; mx 049655-1. Included through the courtesy of RCA Records.

Ellington's *Cotton Tail* is a series of written and improvised variations on the *I Got Rhythm* chord progression (altered slightly in the first chorus, regular thereafter), and it inspired many a surging big band piece during the next decade. Although there are solos by Cootie Williams, Harry Carney, and the leader, it is tenor saxophonist Ben Webster who seems to dominate the piece, and the saxophone section variation that ends it is also his work. Ellington had featured his star soloists in various vehicles and miniature concertos for years, but here, as Gunther Schuller suggests, he seems to have let Webster have a degree of freedom he had never quite granted before.

DUKE ELLINGTON AND HIS FAMOUS ORCHESTRA
In a Mellotone
(Mus., Duke Ellington)
Rec. 9/5/40, Chicago.
Personnel as above.
Soloists: Ellington; Williams; Hodges.
First issue Victor 26788; mx 053428-1. Included through the courtesy of RCA Records.

The most informal of our Ellington selections is this fruitful musical rap on the chord progression of *Rose Room* between the two soloists, Cootie Williams and Johnny Hodges, and the orchestra.

Hodges was one of the great alto saxophonists, a fine bluesman and ballad player in addition to the aspect of his talent heard here.

DUKE ELLINGTON AND HIS FAMOUS ORCHESTRA
Blue Serge
(Mus., Mercer Ellington)
Rec. 2/15/41, Hollywood.
Personnel as directly above except Ray Nance replaces Williams.
Soloists: Bigard (cl); Nance; Ellington; Webster.
First issue Victor 27356; mx 055286-1. Included through the courtesy of RCA Records.

Blue Serge is a beautiful and ingenious treatment of the simplest of all jazz forms, the eight-bar blues. The arrangement may be sketched thus:

Introduction (4 bars): clarinetist Barney Bigard leads, the main theme is alluded to, and then comes a vamp by the trumpets.

First Chorus (8): trumpeter Ray Nance interprets the theme as the trombones continue in accompaniment.

Second Chorus (8 + 2): a thematic variation with brass and reeds variously employed.

Third Chorus (8, unresolved): Nanton's trombone solos, leading directly to

Fourth Chorus: brass with plunger mutes predominates (6) followed by piano solo (2).

Fifth Chorus (8): piano solo continues, restoring the opening theme.

Sixth Chorus (12, or 8 + 4): muted brass into Webster's tenor saxophone solo.

Seventh Chorus (8): a simple, eloquent, beautifully scored ensemble variation on the theme. No true recapitulation.

Ellington, then, has avoided the implicit monotony of his form by setting up a kind of extra two measures, used sparingly (and doubled to four for Webster's solo). He has also tied together the third, fourth, and fifth choruses by leaving out a resolution at the third, and by beginning his own solo two bars "early" in the fourth.

Ending the performance with a sombre thematic variation rather than a recapitulation shows a kind of artistry whose appropriateness comes through to the listener only after he has heard it.

DON BYAS AND SLAM STEWART
I Got Rhythm
(Mus., George Gershwin; lyr., Ira Gershwin)
Rec. 6/9/45.
Don Byas (ts); Slam Stewart (b).
First issue Commodore FL 20029; mx unknown. Included through the courtesy of Commodore Records.

This duo was spontaneously formed when Byas and Stewart were the only performers who had arrived when a Town Hall audience was assembled and ready for a concert. The two men performed *Indiana* and then this arresting exploration of the Gershwin standard.

Byas, in a Hawkins-inspired style in 1945, does everything with this chord progression that a first-rate jazz saxophonist might have done as late as, let's say, 1960. And any listener, musical or not, will be well aware of the creative energy of Byas's solo and of its many surprises.

Stewart was quite well known for his humorous, bowed-and-sung style heard here.

DIZZY GILLESPIE SEXTET
I Can't Get Started

(Mus., Vernon Duke; lyr., Ira Gershwin)
Rec. 1/9/45.
Dizzy Gillespie (t); Trummy Young (tb); Don Byas (ts); Clyde Hart (p); Oscar Pettiford (b); Shelley Manne (d).
Soloist: Gillespie.
First issue Manor 1042; mx W1223. Included through the courtesy of CBS Special Products.

Gillespie's dramatically sustained declamatory exploration of Vernon Duke's ballad is one of those rare performances—an improvisation by a jazzman (and in this case a virtually nonthematic one) that has surprised and delighted the composer of the original.

I Can't Get Started had previously been a successful vehicle for the gifted trumpeter Bunny Berigan, who had succeeded in forming a personal synthesis of the styles of Beiderbecke and Armstrong—succeeded where several others had failed. But from this recording forward, the piece was Gillespie's, and he has recorded it several times since, each with different variations.

DIZZY GILLESPIE ALL STAR QUINTETTE
Shaw 'Nuff

(Mus., Dizzy Gillespie, Charlie Parker)
Arr., Dizzy Gillespie. Rec. 5/11/45.
Dizzy Gillespie (t); Charlie Parker (as); Al Haig (p); Curley Russell (b); Sidney Catlett (d).
Soloists: Haig; Parker; Gillespie; Haig.
First issue Guild 1002; mx 566. Included through the courtesy of Trend Record Corp.

This startling performance might be a classic if only for the superb unison passages between the two hornmen. They seem to enunciate the slightest nuance, even to the "swallowed" notes, as one man. But it has leaping, ebullient, even humorous solos as well. And it offers, full-blown, a new style of jazz.

The title, incidentally, refers to manager and booker Billy Shaw.

CHARLIE PARKER'S RE-BOPPERS
KoKo

(Mus., Charlie Parker)
Rec. 11/26/45.
Charlie Parker (as); Dizzy Gillespie (t, p); Curly Russell (b); Max Roach (d).
Soloists: Gillespie (t); Parker; Roach; Gillespie (t); Parker.
First issue Savoy 597; mx 5853-2. Included through the courtesy of SJ Records.

Suppose one were to invent an ideal jazz soloist as of the early 1940s; what qualities would he need? He would have to have the harmonic exactness of Coleman Hawkins and Don Byas, the harmonic imagination of Art Tatum, and the melodic and rhythmic imagination of Lester Young and Charlie Christian.

But one need not invent such a man, for he existed. His name was Charlie Parker, and his nicknames were "Yardbird" and "Bird."

Actually, he carried the rhythmic message of Young and Christian even further. And he had a power and eloquence comparable to—but quite different from—Louis Armstrong's. He has been called the greatest improvisor jazz has produced. He flashed across the horizon; like any innovator, he was misunderstood, even condemned by some older fans—and a few older musicians. He shed his brilliance and left his influence everywhere and on almost everyone, and then he was dead, in his thirty-fifth year.

KoKo (not Ellington's blues *Ko-Ko,* but one that borrows its chord changes from *Cherokee*) is a torrential, virtuoso improvisation, yet in its use of space, rest, and silence and in its initial juxtaposition of short tension-phrases and flowing, melodious release-phrases, it is also a beautifully paced performance.

Finally, one should not miss the contribution here of Max Roach, already the archetypal bebop drummer.

CHARLIE PARKER WITH JAZZ AT THE PHILHARMONIC
Lady, Be Good

(Mus., George Gershwin; lyr., Ira Gershwin)
Rec. 1/28/46, Los Angeles.
Al Killian, Howard McGhee (t); Charlie Parker,
Willie Smith (as); Lester Young (ts); Arnold
Ross (p); Billy Hadnott (b); Lee Young (d).
Soloists: Ross; Parker.
First issue Disc 2005; mx 245. Included
through the courtesy of PolyGram Records.

Recorded during a concert relatively
early in his career, Charlie Parker's
Lady, Be Good variations are an excellent introduction to his work. He begins
simply, echoing the swing-era playing
that had preceded him, and then enters
the complexities of his own style. His
first four notes are Gershwin's, but he
uses them to introduce a phrase that is
Parker's. His second phrase is a simple
riff. His third alludes to his opening in a
kind of reversed reassortment of its
notes and also incorporates a hint of
that second riff-like phrase. And the patterns of echo and order continue.

Parker's greatness lay not only in the
fertility of his imagination but also in
the compositional integrity of his musical thinking.

CHARLIE PARKER QUINTET
Embraceable You (take #1) [excerpt]

(Mus., George Gershwin; lyr., Ira Gershwin)
Rec. 10/28/47.
Charlie Parker (as); Duke Jordan (p); Tommy
Potter (b); Max Roach (d).
Soloists: Jordan; Parker.
First issue Dial LP 203; mx D 1106 A. Included
through the courtesy of Roulette Records.

Embraceable You (take #2) [excerpt]

Rec. 10/28/47.
Personnel same as above.
Soloists: Jordan; Parker.
First issue Dial 1024; mx D 1106 B. Included
through the courtesy of Spotlite Records.

During a single Dial recording date,
Parker recorded two takes of *Embraceable You,* and either one of them might
rank with his best ballad interpretations.
The first is the best, however, and one
of the most beautifully patterned of all
of his solos. There is one fleeting reference to Gershwin's melody line, but
even it is an integral part of a spontaneous design of Parker's own.

The solo begins simply, and it ends
relatively simply, and its general contours describe a curve upward then
quickly downward. But within the beautiful intricacies of its middle portion,
Parker airs out his more complex
phrases with effectively contrasting simple ones.

The opening motive

is repeated (variously pronounced and
embellished) five times in the first five
bars. But on its fifth appearance, it begins a burst of melody which (one
breath being granted it) comes to rest

with yet another echo of that opening
motive in bars 7 and 8.

From that point on, the motive appears
and reappears in various permutations
as a kind of organizing reference point.
There is an ingenious use of it in bar 18,

and a sequential treatment that begins
after a rest in bar 27.

Such comments are apt to make the
most warm and lyric of ballads seem an
exercise in ingenuity. The ultimate rem-
edy, of course, is to return to the record
itself.

The second version of *Embraceable
You* not only presents a completely different improvisation, it offers a different
kind of overall design. Rather than a rise
and fall, it is a series of peaks and val-
leys, of quick riff-like tension and flowing release.

André Hodeir wrote, "Isn't recognition
of Bird's melodic genius inescapable in
the two versions of *Embraceable You,*
each of which gives new life, in a completely different way, to the Gershwin
theme?"

Charlie Parker circa 1947, a time of peak creativity.

CHARLIE PARKER QUINTET
Klactoveedsedstene
(Mus., Charlie Parker)
Rec. 11/4/47.
Charlie Parker (as); Miles Davis (t); Duke Jordan (p); Tommy Potter (b); Max Roach (d).
Soloists: Roach; Parker; Davis; Jordan; Potter; Roach.
First issue Dial 1040; mx 1112 A. Included through the courtesy of Roulette Records.

The inclusion of this performance by the working group Parker formed in 1947 is perhaps unfair to Miles Davis, who has trouble in his solo. And the weak theme is unworthy of Parker, who gave us *Relaxin' at Camarillo, Moose the Mooche, Scrapple from the Apple, Anthropology,* and *Confirmation.* There are, however, two good reasons for including it and for choosing this take from the two available versions: Parker's fine, suspenseful solo and the superb, varied, interplaying percussion of Max Roach—a definitive statement of bebop, or "modern," drumming and the perfect drum counterpart to Parker's own innovations. From this point on, Roach's drumming became stronger, more authoritative, even more skillful—but, in accompaniment, sometimes more conservative.

[Parker's] solo in Klactoveedsedstene...*is made up of snatches of phrases that sound completely disconnected, even though they follow an implacable logic....*

The melodic discontinuity that we have observed in some of Charlie Parker's choruses is occasionally matched by an equally remarkable rhythmic discontinuity. It sometimes happens, generally in moderate tempos, that the melody and the rhythm are disjointed in a way that verges on the absurd. Snatches of melody then become part of a piecemeal method of phrasing that is surprisingly intense and expressive. The chorus of Klactoveedsedstene *is an excellent example of this approach, in which a rest, becoming part of the phrase's contour, takes on new meaning.* (André Hodeir, *Jazz: Its Evolution and Essence*).

The title here is as it appears on the label of the original release,but it has been otherwise subject to several spellings, several pronunciations, and much speculation on its meaning. Tony Williams of Spotlite Records suggests *Klac-to-Weidersehn*—goodbye to honking, goodbye to noise. Or perhaps the explanation is the simpler one given by a musician: "It's a sound, man. A sound."

CASSETTE SIDE F

CHARLIE PARKER SEXTET
Crazeology (take #1)
(Mus., Benny Harris)
Rec. 12/17/47.
Charlie Parker (as); Miles Davis (t); J.J. Johnson (tb); Duke Jordan (p); Tommy Potter (b); Max Roach (d).
Soloist: Parker.
First issue Dial 1034; mx D 1155-A. Included through the courtesy of Spotlite Records.

Crazeology (take #4)
(Mus., Benny Harris)
Date and personnel as directly above.
Soloists: Parker; Johnson; Davis; Jordan; Potter; Roach; Parker.
First issue Dial LP 207; mx D 1155-D. Included through the courtesy of Roulette Records.

This recording, released under the title *Crazeology* is actually trumpeter Benny Harris's piece *Little Benny*. It features trombonist J.J. Johnson as a guest with Parker's sextet. Johnson was the first to develop a trombone style for modern jazz—actually an adroit, almost abstract, virtuoso style that placed the trombone on the same level as the trumpet and saxophone.

The performance is also something of a minor showpiece for the young Miles Davis in a nicely constructed solo that builds from simplicity to mid-range complexity.

Parker's leaping solo in the second chorus of the performance will surely speak directly to the listener at this point.

The composite version here begins with the opening chorus and solo from the first take of *Crazeology* (which survives only through Parker's full chorus solo) and then moves to the complete fourth take.

CHARLIE PARKER ALL STARS
Parker's Mood
(Mus., Charlie Parker)
Rec. 9/48.
Charlie Parker (as); John Lewis (p); Curly Russell (b); Max Roach (d).
Soloists: Parker; Lewis; Parker; Lewis; Parker; Lewis.
First issue Savoy 936; mx 903-3. Included through the courtesy of SJ Records.

Charlie Parker's sober masterpiece in the slow blues is an ingeniously personal, condensed synthesis of traditional and original fragments.

Also notice John Lewis's fine and almost perfectly complementary episode. He does not break the mood, but his solo is a flow of lyricism in the blues form, with an absolute minimum of blues devices. Those he leaves to Parker.

ERROLL GARNER
Fantasy on Frankie and Johnny
(traditional)
Rec. 6/10/47, Los Angeles.
Erroll Garner (p).
First issue Dial 1026; mx D 1097-A. Included through the courtesy of Roulette Records.

Garner's style was a delightful echo of the swing era in several ways. (His left hand sometimes strums like a 1930s guitar.) An entirely self-taught stylist, he is joyful, puckish, witty, inventive, and always musical. This traditional piece (probably suggested to him as a way to avoid composer royalty complications), which became a kind of instant classic for him, was recorded several years before his playing reached a wide audience. Undoubtedly his imaginative way of using the original melody, of whatever piece he chose to play, helped make that audience a large one.

BUD POWELL TRIO
Night in Tunisia
(Mus., Dizzy Gillespie)
Rec. 5/1/51.
Bud Powell (p); Curly Russell (b); Max Roach (d).
Soloist: Powell.
First issue Blue Note 1576; mx 384. Included through the courtesy of Capitol Records.

By the mid-forties, it was fairly common among insiders to say that Powell on piano was to the modern jazz of the time what Dizzy Gillespie was on trumpet and Charlie Parker on alto saxophone. Musically, he had followed a lead that they provided, to be sure, but to put it that he was "Bird on piano" is to overlook his pianistic heritage, which included an assimilation of (among others) Art Tatum and Teddy Wilson. It is also to overlook his own contributions; his most immediately obvious debt to Parker and Gillespie was that he had absorbed them rhythmically, but clearly he spoke their language with accents and punctuations of his own.

Within a few years some of his ideas had received the...flattery of...popularization by George Shearing. But Powell also received the deeper compliments of a...following among a whole generation of younger pianists. "They cut him up like a gathering of anxious medical students working on a corpse," remarked one player in the early fifties, and many of them took what they could and played it the best they could. Certainly no one equaled the master....

Powell sometimes played like a man running before a threat, and perhaps a part of him knew from the beginning that time would run out for him. There was an urgency in his playing that was sometimes almost extra-musical..., and there was an emphatic precision in his touch, even at the fleetest tempos, that was, and has remained, entirely his own.

Powell's style belonged to the mid-forties, as does his heritage, and the best of his recordings were made by 1953. The great Powell is...the Powell of medium and fast tempo pieces from the

Max Roach. *(Frank Driggs Collection)*

modern repertory or the Powell of standard melodies at similar tempos...What usually mattered in Powell's playing was his finding a basis, almost any basis, for his own inventive, linear energy, an energy that seemed both unabated and, one might say, insatiable.... (Martin Williams, *Jazz Heritage*)

Powell's version of Dizzy Gillespie's *A Night in Tunisia,* a piece through which two generations of musicians tested their prowess, is an excellent demonstration of how well the pianist had learned Parker's lessons of the effective alternation of short, riff-like phrases and flowing inventions, of tension and release—and the bridge in his final chorus is an eight-bar wonder.

RECORD SIDE 9

DEXTER GORDON QUARTET
Bikini
(Mus., Dexter Gordon)
Rec. 6/12/47, Los Angeles.
Dexter Gordon (ts); Jimmy Bunn (p); Red Callender (b); Chuck Thompson (d).
Soloists: Bunn; Gordon; Bunn; Gordon; Thompson; Gordon.
First issue Dial 1022; mx D 1087 A. Included through the courtesy of Spotlite Records.

We have already discussed, in the "Using the Recordings" section, Dexter Gordon's AABA blues in minor; the thing left to underline is Gordon's remarkably undeterred sureness and inventiveness.

Considering the date, the title (which may or may not have been Gordon's) probably refers to the Pacific island where the atomic bomb tests took place, rather than the swimsuit.

TADD DAMERON SEXTET
Lady Bird
(Mus., Tadd Dameron)
Arr., Tadd Dameron. Rec. 9/13/48.
Tadd Dameron (p); Theodore "Fats" Navarro (t); Wardell Gray, Allen Eager (ts); Curly Russell (b); Kenny Clarke (d).
Soloists: Navarro; Eager; Dameron; Gray.
First issue Blue Note 559; mx BN 333-1. Included through the courtesy of Capitol Records.

Fats Navarro's truly gorgeous trumpet solo on this recording shows how far he

had gone beyond absorbing Dizzy Gillespie and into building a style of his own.

Tadd Dameron had written for swing bands in the 1930s before he became an arranger for Gillespie (among others) and the modernists. He also played a kind of "arranger's piano" with groups of his own.

Dameron's delightfully challenging chord progression in *Lady Bird* was subsequently adopted (and slightly modified) for the much-played Miles Davis piece *Half Nelson.*

The two tenor saxophonists here were both, in different degrees, influenced by Lester Young, but Wardell Gray (who has the second tenor solo) had obviously gone further beyond the master than had Allen Eager.

CD IV

MILES DAVIS AND HIS ORCHESTRA
Boplicity
(Mus., "Cleo Henry" [Miles Davis])
Arr., Gil Evans. Rec. 4/22/49.
Miles Davis (t); J.J. Johnson (tb); Sandy Siegelstein (hn); Bill Barber (tba); Lee Konitz (as); Gerry Mulligan (bars); John Lewis (p); Nelson Boyd (b); Kenny Clarke (d).
Soloists: Mulligan; Davis; Lewis.
First issue Capitol 60011; mx 3766-2. Included through the courtesy of Capitol Records.

This ensemble began as a rehearsal band. It had one public engagement, made a few recordings, and disappeared, but its influence was widespread and sustained.

The "cool jazz" of the 1950s was chiefly the work of this group and of Lennie Tristano, Lee Konitz, Gerry Mulligan, and a group of tenor saxophonists, all of whom were indebted in various ways to Lester Young. The most prominent of those saxophonists was Stan Getz.

Boplicity was an early collaboration of Davis and arranger Gil Evans. Evans's abilities in giving properly sonorous settings to the trumpeter's glowingly detached, yet paradoxically forceful, style were exceptional. Here, the interplay between Davis and the group is excellently planned and executed. Davis subsequently expressed dissatisfaction with the melody of *Boplicity,* but not with its harmonic structure nor with Evans's treatment.

André Hodeir, in *Jazz: Its Evolution and Essence,* discusses that treatment in some detail, particularly the way Evans has effectively broken down the eight-bar phrases of song form. The performance contains two AABA choruses, but the first chorus ends on an A section of nine and a half bars, and the bridge of the second chorus is a deceptively fluent four-plus-two-plus-four bars.

LENNIE TRISTANO QUINTET
Subconscious Lee
(Mus., Lee Konitz)
Rec. 1/11/49.
Lee Konitz (as); Lennie Tristano (p); Billy Bauer (g); Arnold Fishkin (b); Shelly Manne (d).
Soloists: Tristano; Bauer; Konitz; Tristano; Bauer; Konitz; Tristano.
First issue New Jazz 80001; mx JRC8. Included through the courtesy of Fantasy Records.

In his notes to the Capitol LP *Crosscurrents* (M11060), collecting the seven selections Lennie Tristano and his associates recorded for that label, Dutch critic Martin Schowten wrote:

Cool, that's what used to be the catchword. Paralleling the exciting developments of Charlie Parker and the boppers, Lennie's select coterie of musicians developed a low-temperature approach to jazz improvisation. Unusual and exciting harmonic and rhythmic twists were rare in the pure Tristano style, which was based largely on the construction of flowing melodic lines that swept across the normally accepted breaks in phrasing. In terms of the dynamic level, nothing much was allowed to happen and the rhythm section was only to play a time-keeping role. The drummers had to play brushes on their snare drum, with a completely even attack throughout....The bass player had to follow the same procedure....So listeners' attention is focused on the melody....But the schoolmasterish attitude had its positive aspect....

These seven Tristano sides are an important footnote to jazz history, because of their influence and because of the playing of two brilliant musicians [Konitz and Tristano]. Because of the theoretical implications and the integrity of the music, with its boy-scoutlike whistling-in-the-morning-feeling.

Subconscious Lee—actually variations on Cole Porter's *What Is This Thing Called Love?*—is Konitz's choice for his own work from among his recorded collaborations with Tristano.

One other note: two of the recordings from the Capitol series, *Digression* and *Intuition,* were free improvisations performed with no preconceptions as to melody, chords, tempo, or mood. Thus they predicted the jazz of the 1960s.

GENE NORMAN'S "JUST JAZZ" FEATURING RED NORVO AND STAN GETZ
Body and Soul [excerpt]
(Mus., Johnny Green; lyr., Robert Sauer, Ed Heyman, Frank Eyton)
Rec. 6/23/47, Pasadena.
Charlie Shavers (t); Willie Smith (as); Stan Getz (ts); Red Norvo (vib); Nat "King" Cole (p); Oscar Moore (elec g); Johnnie Miller (b); Louis Bellson (d).
Soloists: Norvo; Getz; Moore; Cole.
First issue Modern 20-695; mx MM990 & MM991. Included through the courtesy of GNP Crescendo Record Co.

Red Norvo began his career on the xylophone. He switched to the vibraharp in the 1940s but played the instrument without the electric vibrators turned on, as though it were a metal xylophone. His arpeggio-oriented style and his harmonically knowledgeable musicianship carried this remarkable performer from the mid-1930s forward. His widest popularity came in the 1950s, when he led a trio featuring guitar (Tal Farlow, later Jimmy Raney) and bass (Charles Mingus, later Red Mitchell).

In this live concert performance, I have omitted the opening chorus and gone directly to Norvo's half-chorus. Stan Getz's brief, poignant bridge, beautiful and singularly self-contained, is an ideal introduction to the melancholy lyr-

Sarah Vaughan at work. *(Photo by Charles Stewart)*

icism and unique saxophone sound of his ballad playing. Then the King Cole Trio enters, with the pianist and his guitarist, Oscar Moore, in a performance that serves to remind us of the timelessness of Cole's early work as a jazz pianist.

SARAH VAUGHAN
All Alone
(Mus. & lyr., Irving Berlin)
Arr., Thad Jones. Rec. 1967.
Sarah Vaughan (voc); Clark Terry, Charlie Shavers, Joe Newman, Freddie Hubbard (t); J.J. Johnson, Kai Winding (tb); Phil Woods, Benny Golson (reeds); Bob James (p).
First issue Mercury SR 61116; mx unknown. Included through the courtesy of PolyGram Records.

My Funny Valentine
(Mus., Richard Rodgers; lyr., Lorenz Hart)
Rec. 9/24/73, Tokyo.
Sarah Vaughan (voc); Carl Schroeder (p).
First issue Mainstream 2401; mx unknown. Included through the courtesy of Audiofidelity Enterprises, Inc.

One of the most remarkable of American singers,...Sarah Vaughan has one of the biggest and most powerful voices—in range, in volume, in body, in variety of texture, in flexibility—that our...music has ever seen. Indeed...you may come away convinced that hers is a voice, and a control and use of a voice, that is quite beyond category or style.

[There is also] a starkly dramatic side of her talent that is all but unexpected. More often Sarah Vaughan the singer seems to regard experience with the precocious stance of a worldly and witty Alice in an adult Wonderland, accepting the foibles and pretenses of adults only through the act of doubting them....

Sarah Vaughan can, like a good jazz instrumentalist, improvise a totally new melody within an harmonic outline....[She] can jump wide intervals at full volume and come down on an unexpected note with precision. She can go up to the top of her range and squeeze a note, or bend and shake a note right out of the bottom of her range— practices which would tear many an untrained voice, and many a trained one, to shreds. (Martin Williams, "Sarah

Vaughan: Some Notes on a Singer Before It's Too Late," in *Evergreen Review* #42)

And Vaughan uses her variable (and fully controlled) vibrato—or rather range of vibrati—as a careful ornament rather than a constant.

Here her developing sense of drama and her interplay with the orchestra serve her well, as she turns Irving Berlin's early, sentimental waltz, *All Alone,* into a sly plea for company, and Rodgers and Hart's tender eulogy, *My Funny Valentine,* a challenging example of songwriting in the first place, into an exploratory tour de force displaying all her vocal resources.

RECORD SIDE 10

CASSETTE SIDE G

THELONIOUS MONK QUARTET
Misterioso
(Mus., Thelonious Monk)
Arr., Thelonious Monk. Rec. 7/2/48.
Thelonious Monk (p); Milt Jackson (vib); John Simmons (b); Shadow Wilson (d).
Soloists: Monk; Jackson; Monk.
First issue Blue Note 560; mx BN 329. Included through the courtesy of Capitol Records.

Misterioso is a classic Thelonious Monk blues, and the performance here shows that the composer-pianist's sense of form, although no less authentic than, say, Morton's or Ellington's, is more improvisational.

The recording opens with the theme, based on what jazz musicians call walking sixths, stated by Monk and vibraphonist Milt Jackson, while string bass and drums phrase along with them. With the second chorus, the latter two instruments begin their regular rhythmic-harmonic 1-2-3-4, and Jackson a fine blues man, begins to improvise. For his accompaniment, however, Monk does not play blues chords as another pianist might do. He plays around with the "blue seventh," the next implied note of his theme, so to speak, as if to say, "This is not just the blues in this key. It is a particular piece of mine called *Misterioso.*"

During his own subsequent solo, Monk echoes the upward, walking movement of this theme. (He also adds an extra bar to the first chorus of his solo, intentionally or not.) In the final chorus, as Jackson recapitulates the theme, Monk meanwhile counterpoints a kind of aired-out version of his previous accompaniment, echoes his solo, and finally joins Jackson's final few notes of the recapitulation. Thus, the composer makes the last chorus a kind of semi-improvised summary of the entire performance.

Monk recorded *Misterioso* several times, including another take on Blue Note done at the same record date by the same ensemble. It is not the equal of this version, but the differences are instructive on the nature of Monk's music and jazz.

THELONIOUS MONK QUARTET
Evidence

(Mus., Thelonious Monk)
Arr., Thelonious Monk. Rec. 7/2/48.
Thelonious Monk (p); Milt Jackson (vib); John Simmons (b); Shadow Wilson (d).
Soloists: Monk; Jackson; Monk and Jackson.
First issue Blue Note 549; mx BN 328. Included through the courtesy of Capitol Records.

With Evidence, *a little hindsight is an advantage; that is, the recording is even better if we know Monk's melody, at least in its later manifestations. Here it appears in [his] introduction, darts in and out of [his] relatively conventional solo. Then, at the end of the performance, in the interplay between Monk and Jackson, this apparently jagged, disparate, intriguing tissue of related sounds has at last emerged, but not quite—a theme of great strength and almost classic beauty for all its asymmetry and surprise.* (Martin Williams, "Thelonious Monk: Modern Jazz In Search of Maturity" in *The Jazz Tradition*)

THELONIOUS MONK QUINTET
Criss-Cross

(Mus., Thelonious Monk)
Arr., Thelonious Monk. Rec. 7/23/51.
Thelonious Monk (p); Edmond Gregory [Sahib Shihab] (as); Milt Jackson (vib); Al McKibbon (b); Art Blakey (d).
Soloists: Monk; Jackson; Gregory; Monk.
First issue Blue Note 1590; mx BN 393. Included through the courtesy of Capitol Records.

Criss-Cross...*stands out as perhaps the Monk masterpiece of this period. It contains all the by now familiar melodic-harmonic characteristics, his innovations in shifting rhythms and accents, but is above all important because it is a purely instrumental conception. It is not a "song", a term so many jazz musicians apply to all the music they work with, it is not a "tune"—it is a composition for instruments. But its most radical aspect is that* Criss-Cross *is in a sense an abstraction. It does not describe or portray anything specific, it does not attempt to set a "mood" or the like; it simply states and develops certain musical ideas, in much the way that an abstract painter will work with specific nonobjective patterns.* (Gunther Schuller, "Thelonious Monk" in *Jazz Panorama*)

THELONIOUS MONK
Bag's Groove [solo from Miles Davis's All Stars recording]

(Mus., Milt Jackson)
Rec. 12/24/54.
Thelonious Monk (p); Percy Heath (b); Kenny Clarke (d).
Soloist: Monk.
First issue Prestige LP 7109; mx 676-? Included through the courtesy of Fantasy Records.

This excerpt comes from a consistently high-level recording date that also included Davis, as the all-star date's leader, and Milt Jackson.

Monk's own solo, deceptively simple on the surface perhaps, is one of the great moments of recorded jazz. Pianist Dick Katz has written in Jazz Panorama *that "by an ingenious use of space and rhythm, and by carefully controlling a* single melodic idea, he builds tension that is not released until the end of his solo....His sense of structure and his use of extension is very rare indeed. And it sounds good." André Hodeir speaks, in Toward Jazz, of the "tremendous pressure" which Monk, in his disjunct phrasing and pregnant silences exerts on his listeners. And Hodeir even singles out the detail of the "shattering" effect in Monk's first chorus of the F-sharp that follows the series of C's and F's—"one of the purest moments of beauty in the history of jazz."

And the solo as a whole is one of the most prophetic, I would add. It does not so much link ideas, one to the next, as Davis did, as it airily spins out of itself, out of its own opening phrase—as both Katz and Hodeir indicate. And, although one could readily tick off the number of blues choruses involved, the solo virtually floats above its chord changes and their implied 4-bar phrases, determining its own character as it goes along. Indeed in 1954, Monk outlined the major tasks of the new jazz of the 1960s. (Martin Williams, liner notes for *Miles Davis and the Modern Jazz Giants*, Prestige 7650)

The one element in Monk's music that is somewhat covert in the selections included here is his humor, which is overt in his fine, somewhat sardonic 1956 trio versions of *Honeysuckle Rose* and, particularly, *Tea for Two*.

THELONIOUS MONK
I Should Care

(Mus., Paul Weston, Axel Stordahl; lyr., Sammy Cahn)
Rec. 4/12/57.
Thelonious Monk (p).
First issue Riverside RLP 12-235; mx unknown. Included through the courtesy of Fantasy Records.

From Gunther Schuller, "Thelonious Monk" in *Jazz Panorama*:

Unhampered by other players and beholden only unto himself, Monk ruminates thoughtfully and caressingly in free tempo. Monk makes these tunes completely his own, continually extracting and paring down to the essence of

each melody and harmony. They all have a beauty and haunting lyricism, especially April in Paris, I Should Care, and All Alone. Other adjectives that come to mind are "mournful" and "nostalgic." I Should Care is worth many rehearings, as Monk toward the end— after a sort of private double-time passage—plays four chords in which, after first striking all the notes hard and sharply, he quickly releases all but one. This kind of chord distillation is one of the most radical aspects of his music, i.e., the idea that one note above all others can most succinctly represent a chord—not a new idea in music, but almost untried in jazz. In the last half of I Should Care Monk is especially exciting in terms of free tempo playing. His arhythmic, unexpected moves create a tremendous tension.

From André Hodeir, "Monk or the Misunderstood" in *Toward Jazz*:

It is not hard to see why I am so fascinated by [Monk's] remarkable I Should Care....It consists of a series of impulses which disregard the bar line completely, pulverize the musical tissue and yet preserve intact..."jazz feeling."...These elongations of musical time....Is it so unreasonable to think that they exist as a function of a second, underlying tempo, imperceptible to us but which Monk hears in all the complexity of its relationships with the figures he is playing?

One may wonder what remains of the theme of I Should Care after this acid bath, and in fact, of the ballad in general, considered an essential element of jazz sensibility. Personally, I am delighted at this transmutation, which is in keeping with the breath of fresh air brought to jazz, in my opinion, by [Monk's] own original themes.

HORACE SILVER QUINTET
Moon Rays

(Mus., Horace Silver)
Arr., Horace Silver. Rec. 1/13/58.
Horace Silver (p); Art Farmer (t); Clifford Jordan (ts); Teddy Kotick (b); Louis Hayes (d).
Soloists: Jordan; Farmer; Silver.
First issue Blue Note BLP 1589; mx unknown. Included through the courtesy of Capitol Records.

Miles Davis and Gil Evans.

In their fine craftsmanship Horace Silver's quintets, along with Art Blakey's Jazz Messengers, virtually defined the hard bop style of the 1950s and afterward, and Silver particularly the "funky" version of it (i.e., lots of blue notes).

Moon Rays, however, a somewhat neglected piece, is almost ballad-like in its character and tempo. It does show the leader guiding his soloists and filling in almost orchestrally from his piano, and it has a particularly attractive secondary theme. It also features a superb, unfolding solo by Art Farmer.

RECORD SIDE 11

MILES DAVIS WITH GIL EVANS'S ORCHESTRA
Summertime

(Mus., George Gershwin; lyr., DuBose Heywood)
Arr., Gil Evans. Rec. in stereo 8/18/58.
Miles Davis (t); John Coles, Bernie Glow, Ernie Royal, Louis Mucci (t); Joe Bennett, Frank Rehak, Jimmy Cleveland (tb); Dick Hixon (btb); Willie Ruff, Julius Watkins, Gunther Schuller (hn); Bill Barber (tba); Julian "Cannonball" Adderley (as); Phil Bodner, Romeo Penque (fl); Danny Bank (bcl); Paul Chambers (b); Jimmy Cobb (d); Gil Evans (dir).
Soloist: Davis.
First issue Columbia CS 8085; mx CO 61421.
Included through the courtesy of CBS Special Products.

Summertime was the most popularly successful piece (and possibly the simplest) from the third important collaboration of Evans and Davis (the second was the album *Miles Ahead*). That collaboration was built around the themes from George Gershwin's *Porgy and Bess.*

This performance takes the familiar lullaby at an unexpected medium tempo and in an almost jaunty mood, yet Davis's inventive paraphrase and improvisation on the theme is wholly compelling and convincing. The various treatments, in scoring and voicing, that Evans gives his accompanying riff—his use of the sonorous resources of his orchestra—show skill and a craftmanship of a very high order. Together, Davis and Evans have recomposed *Summertime* into a new work. Davis's solo will also reveal why he has been compared to Louis Armstrong, and why his modern style was called a traditional one brought up to date by his harmonic and rhythmic sensitivity.

CHARLES MINGUS QUINTET
Haitian Fight Song
(Mus., Charles Mingus)
Arr., Charles Mingus. Rec. 3/12/57.
Jimmy Knepper (tb); Curtis Porter [Shafi Hadi] (as); Wade Legge (p); Charles Mingus (b); Danny Richmond (d).
Soloists: Mingus, Knepper; Legge; Porter; Mingus; Knepper.
First issue Atlantic LP 1260; mx 2458. Included through the courtesy of Warner Special Products, Inc.

Charles Mingus's recordings make for difficult choices. He was an outstanding bassist—a rare soloist regardless of instrument—and he was the man who moved the bass out of its strictly accompanying role by providing interplaying polyphonic lines that made him an almost equal participant with the horns. He was also an outstanding composer and ensemble leader.

Haitian Fight Song is worthy evidence of at least two of his contributions, those of bass soloist and composer. It is also a programmatically appropriate piece for Mingus's often turbulent musical personality. A later recording (some-

how retitled *II B.S.*) has a more polished reading of the piece—and a plunger-muted trumpet in place of Mingus's vocal part here. But it lacks the fire of this one, and the leader's bass work is less outstanding.

One might next recommend to the listener such examples of Mingus the composer and bassist as *Pithecanthropus Erectus*; *Moanin'*; *Goodbye Pork Pie Hat*; *E's Flat, Ah's Flat Too*; and *Fables of Faubus,*—but his counterpoint duet with Eric Dolphy's alto saxophone on *Stormy Weather* is a masterpiece.

CASSETTE SIDE H

MODERN JAZZ QUARTET
Django
(Mus., John Lewis)
Arr., John Lewis. Rec. in stereo 4/12/60, Gothenburg, Sweden.
Milt Jackson (vib); John Lewis (p); Percy Heath (b); Connie Kay (d).
Soloists: Jackson; Lewis; Jackson.
First issue Atlantic 2-603; mx 4816. Included through the courtesy of Warner Special Products, Inc.

Lewis as composer and musical director, and Jackson, Lewis, Heath, and Kay as players arrived at a spontaneous and yet structured group music,....

Django is perhaps John Lewis' finest work as a composer and finest achievement in form as musical director of the Quartet. The piece is...a funeral processional for the Belgian gypsy guitarist-turned-jazzman, Django Reinhardt. Its main melody seems to imply all that—a French-Belgian, gypsy, and jazz elegy. But the performance demonstrates that there was something else in Lewis's mind as well—the tradition in New Orleans culture, and in early jazz, of consolation and rejoicing at death, of funeral processions with musicians who offer both reverent hymns of mourning and redeeming songs of joy. The improvised choruses, on Lewis's unusual structure, are interrupted by a lively blues bass figure, almost as old as jazz, which reappears and gradually converts the players from their introspection. In the end, there is a kind of resolution between the opposing moods of sadness and joy as the main theme re-enters.

Django *is one of the few truly sustained "extended" performances in recorded jazz. The subtle range of feeling it encompasses would be an achievement all by itself. Its melodies and motives are excellent, being both original and traditional, and these, along with its harmonic structure, have the mandatory quality of good jazz composition—they inspire good solos.* (Martin Williams, liner notes to *The Modern Jazz Quartet Plays Jazz Classics,* Prestige 7425)

SONNY ROLLINS PLUS FOUR
Pent-Up House [abridged]
(Mus., Sonny Rollins)
Rec. in stereo 3/22/56, Hackensack NJ
Sonny Rollins (ts); Clifford Brown (t); Richie Powell (p); George Morrow (b); Max Roach (d).
Soloists: Brown; Rollins; Powell; Roach.
First issue Prestige LP 7038; mx 868. Included through the courtesy of Fantasy Records.

Dizzy Gillespie has said that trumpeter Clifford Brown was working on the things that Fats Navarro didn't get from him.

This group is actually the celebrated Max Roach–Clifford Brown Quintet, recording here for a rival label under Rollins's name. Thus we have virtuoso Rollins in addition to Brown's sunny, quick, fluent virtuosity. And the trading of twos (two-bar phrases) at the end should delight any listener. (The selection is abridged, in that I have shortened the piano solo.)

Brown's last recordings, authentic jam session tapes made just before his shockingly early death in 1956, have been issued, and among them his *Night in Tunisia* solo is almost overwhelmingly inventive.

RECORD SIDE 12
CD V

SONNY ROLLINS QUARTET
Blue 7
(Mus., Sonny Rollins)

Rec. 6/22/56.
Sonny Rollins (ts); Tommy Flanagan (p); Doug Watkins (b); Max Roach (d).
Soloists: Watkins; Rollins; Flanagan; Roach; Rollins; Flanagan; Watkins; Rollins and Roach; Rollins.
First issue Prestige LP 7079; mx 921. Included through the courtesy of Fantasy Records.

I think you sense the importance of this music immediately, as you sense the sureness and the authority of almost every phrase that Sonny Rollins plays here. You hear the combination of power and ease in his horn, and you know that the promising young tenor player has become a masterful jazz musician.

But there is more to it than that. Besides the emotional impact, there is an acute musical intelligence at work here, and the performances represent a rare combination of spontaneous feeling and musical thoughtfulness, of emotional immediacy and affirmative order.

Inevitably the growing musical maturity of the Sonny Rollins of mid-1956 is not without its basis in the facts of Sonny Rollins's personal life. This LP was made when Rollins was a member of the Clifford Brown–Max Roach quintet. He had joined the group a few months earlier in Chicago at the climax of a period of rigorous self-assessment and personal and musical discipline, reflection, and study....

Then Blue 7. *A masterpiece. Like most masterpieces it is difficult to describe and discuss; it seems to have a life of its own and one never hears it without hearing something wonderfully new in it. Its heritage—beginning with Thelonious Monk's blues* Misterioso *and going through* Vierd Blues *which Rollins recorded with Miles Davis...—is certainly worth noting, but* Blue 7 *also exists entirely on its own.*

It opens with a quiet, almost noncommittal walk from Doug Watkins's bass. Then Rollins enters for the theme—

Sonny Rollins in the early 1970s.

simple, yet firm and very much committed. And technically quite intriguing by the way, for it is ambiguous—it might be in either of two keys or both. Flanagan's entry firms it down, and from this point on its implicit brilliance is expertly explored.

Blue 7 is one of those rare improvised performances in which every part is related to every other part,...with details so subtle and perfectly in place that it might take a composer hours to arrive at—yet Rollins made it all up in a recording studio as he went along. It is as if Rollins conceived of Blue 7 as a whole all at once, although we hear him building it logically, from one phrase to the next.

The key is, as Max Roach once said, Thelonious Monk's admonition: Why don't we use the melody? Why do we throw it away after the first chorus and just use the chords?

But using the melody involves a lot more than simple decorations and embellishments. Almost everything that Sonny Rollins plays here is ingeniously based on the opening theme of Blue 7. But Rollins, like Monk, can get inside a melody, elaborate it logically, or reduce it to a tantalizing tissue of notes, an essence, and rebuild it once more from that outline—Rollins can even build on his elaborations and interpolations.

But the order and logic on Blue 7 do not all belong to Rollins. Max Roach's assertive portion is subtly built around a triplet figure and a roll, both of which he states early in his solo....Thus for all its subtlety Blue 7 is the kind of performance that almost anyone grasps immediately. That is, it is the kind of performance to use on the middle-aged uncle who wants to know, 'Where's the melody in jazz?' It is also the kind of performance to use in introducing jazz to a complete newcomer. And at the same time it is the kind of performance one might use on the most sophisticated musician to show how excellent jazz improvisation can be. (Martin Williams, liner notes to Saxophone Colossus, Prestige 7326)

WES MONTGOMERY QUARTET
West Coast Blues [abridged]
(Mus., Wes Montgomery)
Arr., Wes Montgomery. Rec. in stereo 1/26 or 28/60.
Tommy Flanagan (p); Wes Montgomery (g); Percy Heath (b); Albert Heath (d).
Soloist: Montgomery.
First issue Riverside RLP12-320; mx unknown. Included through the courtesy of Fantasy Records.

Listeners will probably discern from Oscar Moore's work on Body and Soul that Moore admired Django Reinhardt. And Jimmy Raney made a fleet electric guitar style under the spell of Charlie Parker's alto saxophone. But our previous generalization that Charlie Christian's effect on jazz guitarists was dominant for two decades is valid. However, the arrival of Wes Montgomery changed that.

His West Coast Blues, in addition to its other virtues, is metrically tantalizing. The opening and closing theme establishes a 6/8 waltz, and then Montgomery's solo moves to 3/4, but the accompaniment and some of Montgomery's own phrases set up a tension in the direction of a jazz 4/4.

His solo is also a structural wonder, from single-line blues improvisations, through block chords imitated by guitar octaves, to a full-chorded section.

MILES DAVIS SEXTET
So What
(Mus., Miles Davis)
Arr., Miles Davis. Rec. in stereo 3/2/59.
Miles Davis (t); John Coltrane (ts); Julian "Cannonball" Adderley (as); Bill Evans (p); Paul Chambers (b); James Cobb (d).
Soloists: Evans; Chambers; Davis; Coltrane; Adderley; Evans; Chambers.
First issue Columbia CS 8163; mx CO 62290. Included through the courtesy of CBS Special Products.

This selection from the LP Kind of Blue discussed earlier is remarkable for the sense of clarity and release that each of the players finds in his solo.

More will be said below about the career of John Coltrane. It was soon after this association with Davis that the formidable Cannonball Adderley went on to form his own groups and achieve worldwide popularity. The pianist here is Bill Evans, of whom Davis once said that when he played a chord it wasn't a collection of notes but a sound.

Davis further explored the modal idiom on LPs like *Miles Smiles* and *Sorcerer*, all of them also notable for the contributions of several other musicians, including the innovative drummer Tony Williams.

RECORD SIDE 13

CASSETTE SIDE I

BILL EVANS TRIO
Blue in Green
(Mus., Bill Evans, Miles Davis)
Arr., Bill Evans. Rec. in stereo 12/28/59.
Bill Evans (p); Scott LaFaro (b); Paul Motian (d).
Soloist: Evans.
First issue Riverside RLP12-315; mx unknown.
Included through the courtesy of Fantasy Records.

Blue in Green is an unusually structured ten-measure piece on a harmonic sequence suggested to Bill Evans by Miles Davis; a version of it is included in the *Kind of Blue* LP. Here it introduces the Evans Trio which was, as its leader intended, not a pianist accompanied by bass and drums but three equal participants inventing together.

Evans's harmonic language, his practice of voicing his chords without their root notes, opened up the possibilities for a whole generation of successor pianists, including Keith Jarrett, Chick Corea, Herbie Hancock, and others. On the intrinsic merit of his work and on the high quality of his lyricism and his influence, Evans held a position in recent jazz history comparable to Beiderbecke's in the 1920s and 1930s.

CECIL TAYLOR UNIT
Enter Evening
(Mus., Cecil Taylor)
Arr., Cecil Taylor. Rec. in stereo 6/16/66.
Cecil Taylor (p, bells); Eddie Gale Stevens, Jr. (t); Jimmy Lyons (as); Ken McIntyre (ob); Henry Grimes, Alan Silva (b); Andrew Cyrille (d).
First issue Blue Note 84237; mx unknown.
Included through the courtesy of Capitol Records.

In the liner notes of his Looking Ahead *(Contemporary) record Taylor said: "Everything I've lived, I am. I am not afraid of European influences. The point is to use them—as Ellington did—as part of my life as an American Negro...."*

Cecil Taylor is not ashamed of his conservatory background. (Cecil told Joe Goldberg: "I like hell am [conservatory trained]. If my musical training stopped when I left the conservatory, you wouldn't be talking to me now....")

Cecil believes that his problem is to utilize the energies of the European composers, their technique, consciously, and blend this with the traditional music of the American Negro, and to create a new energy. And was it unique? "No. Historically not. This is what has always happened. Ellington did it."

Bob Levin quotes Cecil in his notes to the Hard Driving Jazz *record as saying: "The object of any jazz musician who has had [my] background is to bring it to jazz—combine it with jazz and see what happens. My particular field is jazz and therefore it will eventually become a complete jazz expression. I think it is right for any would-be artist to try and get material from as many places as possible."* (A.B. Spellman, *Four Lives in the Bebop Business*)

Taylor's influences here (Stravinsky, Ellington, Monk) are identifiable but assimilated, and the result is a remarkably realized performance of a Cecil Taylor work for jazzmen, *Enter Evening*. Hear, for example, the individuality of sound and interpretation that Taylor requires of the musicians, or the way he "conducts," animates, from the impulses of his keyboard.

JOHN COLTRANE QUARTET
Alabama

(Mus., John Coltrane)
Arr., John Coltrane. Rec. in stereo 11/18/63.
John Coltrane (ts); McCoy Tyner (p); Jimmy
Garrison (b); Elvin Jones (d).
Soloist: Coltrane.
First issue Impulse AS-50; mx unknown. In-
cluded through the courtesy of MCA Records.

John Coltrane's music, after his asso-
ciations with Miles Davis and
Thelonious Monk, took two directions.
Pieces like *Countdown* and *Giant Steps*
(etudes, one might say) had challenging,
densely structured chord progressions,
but pieces like *Impressions* and the extended *A Love Supreme* were chordless
and modal. And the penultimate *Ascension* was entirely "free" and executed
under the influence of Ornette Coleman.

Alabama begins as if with solemn
meditation, moves to prayer, to hope, to
affirmation, and ends again in prayer.
When asked if it concerned the desegre-
gation problems of its date and the
bombing deaths of some black children
in Alabama, Coltrane replied simply, "It
represents, musically, something that I
saw down there, translated into music
from inside me."

ORNETTE COLEMAN QUARTET
Lonely Woman

(Mus., Ornette Coleman)
Arr., Ornette Coleman. Rec. in stereo 5/22/59,
Los Angeles.
Ornette Coleman (as); Donald Cherry (t);
Charlie Haden (b); Billy Higgins (d).
Soloist: Coleman.
First issue Atlantic SD 1317; mx 3511. In-
cluded through the courtesy of Warner Spe-
cial Products, Inc.

RECORD SIDE 14

CASSETTE SIDE J

Congeniality

(Mus., Ornette Coleman)
Arr., Ornette Coleman. Rec. in stereo 5/22/59,
Los Angeles.
Personnel as above.
Soloists: Coleman; Cherry.
First issue Atlantic SD 1317; mx 3510. In-
cluded through the courtesy of Warner Spe-
cial Products, Inc.

The passion of Ornette Coleman's
music is immediately evident, and
Lonely Woman, perhaps the most powerful of a series of magnificent dirges
that he recorded, is one of his most
compelling and disturbing recordings.
The beginning, with bass and drums in
counter-rhythm, followed by the trumpet
and alto sax, obliquely intoned, entering
at a most unexpected place and at a
most unexpected tempo—this alone
announces Coleman's originality, and his
exploratory solo expounds on it.

The quite different mood of *Congeniality* (an exceptionally well-named
piece) also illustrates the logical discipline and sequential nature of Coleman's
improvising. As one motive appears it is
turned, developed, elaborated, or condensed until it yields another of itself, or
yields to a different motive from
Coleman's imagination. (This solo is discussed in detail by Gunther Schuller in
his book *Musings*.)

The dense ensemble procedures are
aharmonic. Charlie Haden's bass moves
almost as a melodically free agent behind Coleman and Cherry, for example.
But such things are not matters of a
lack of discipline; they are effectively
deliberate parts of a unique musical
purpose.

Three quotations from Ornette Coleman:

"If I'm going to follow a preset chord
sequence, I may as well write out my
solo."

"You can play sharp in tune and flat
in tune," and he elaborates that a D in a
context depicting sadness should not
sound the same as a D in a passage of
joy.

"It was when I found out that I could
make mistakes that I knew I was onto
something."

Ornette Coleman.

ORNETTE COLEMAN DOUBLE QUARTET
Free Jazz [excerpt]
(Mus., Ornette Coleman)
Arr., Ornette Coleman. Rec. in stereo 12/21/60.
Ornette Coleman (as); Donald Cherry, Freddie Hubbard (t); Eric Dolphy (bcl); Scott LaFaro, Charlie Haden (b); Billy Higgins, Ed Blackwell (d).
First issue Atlantic S-1364; mx 5247. Included through the courtesy of Warner Special Products.

This excerpt presents Coleman's section of an extraordinary thirty-six minute improvisation by the double quartet listed above. It is in some ways the most impressive portion. The hambone beat set up behind Coleman is perhaps kept up too long—although it does serve to emphasize the fundamental and earthly aspect of his work. ("Ornette Coleman plays field hollers," is bass player and museum director Julian Euell's complimentary description.)

Ornette Coleman's style...has never been realized as it is here. Nor tested as it is here, for I don't suppose any jazz performance ever took bigger chances. Not only is the improvisation almost total, it is frequently collective, involving all eight men inventing at once. And there were no preconceptions as to themes, chord patterns, or chorus lengths. The guide for each soloist was a brief ensemble part which introduced him and which gave him an area of musical pitch. Otherwise he had only feelings and imagination—his own and those of his accompanists—to guide him. Ornette Coleman put it, "We were expressing our minds and emotions as much as could be captured by electronics."

Coleman has said that one of the basic ideas in his music is to encourage the improviser to be freer, and not obey a preconceived chord-pattern according to set ideas of "proper" harmony and tonality: "Let's try to play the music and not the background." However, his point is basically emotional and aesthetic, not technical. The music should be a direct and immediate "expressing our minds and our emotions rather than being a background for emotion....Often the "solo" here is (as in much New Orleans jazz) an exchange of the lead players. "The most important thing," says Coleman, "was for us to play together, all at the same time, without getting in each other's way, and also to have enough room for each player to ad lib alone—and to follow his idea for the duration of the album. When the soloist played something that suggested a musical idea or direction to me, I played that behind him in my style. He continued his own way in his solo, of course." A kind of polyphonic accompaniment based on pitch, melodic direction, an emotional complement, then. (Martin Williams, liner notes to *Free Jazz*, Atlantic S-1364)

The one aspect of the work of Coleman and his ensembles not covered in our selections is spontaneous group changes in tempo, which can be heard in *The Riddle*, and *Antiques*.

WORLD SAXOPHONE QUARTET
Steppin'

(Mus., Julius Hemphill)
Rec. in stereo 11/6/81, Zurich.
Hamiet Bluiett (afl); Julius Hemphill, Oliver Lake (ss); David Murray (bcl).
First issue Black Saint 0077; mx unknown.
Included through the courtesy of IREC.

At this stage of their career, the World Saxophone Quartet makes for difficult choices, because no one or two of their recordings can show all of their virtues. *Steppin',* for example, has David Murray, already a major jazz tenor saxophonist, playing only bass clarinet, and Hamiet Bluiett on alto flute rather than baritone, with Hemphill (who has become the group's chief composer) and Lake both on sopranos only. And the nature and extent of written theme, played a twelfth apart by Murray and Bluiett, is untypically clear here, and clearly distinguished from the improvised section.

But this live version of *Steppin'* has many obvious virtues, not the least of which is the immediately evident passion of the group's music. And the simultaneous improvising shows a quick mutual understanding among the players that rivals King Oliver's Creole Jazz Band and produces an effective polyphonic texture in which there seems not a wasted phrase or note. In the World Saxophone Quartet, after over twenty exploratory years, the jazz once called the new thing has found its maturity.

—*Martin Williams*

Biographical Index

LOUIS ARMSTRONG

(1900, New Orleans–1971)
Armstrong started in music at age seven, singing in the streets for coins with a group of his friends. On New Year's Eve 1912 he fired a gun by way of celebration and was arrested and sent to the Colored Waifs' Home, where he learned to play the cornet. After his release he came under the influence of King Oliver, and in 1922 Oliver asked Armstrong to join him in Chicago as second cornet. Louis's obvious talent began to attract attention.

In 1924 he joined Fletcher Henderson's orchestra in New York and became the envy of countless trumpeters and other instrumentalists. His influence continued and expanded on an international level as a result of his Hot Five and Hot Seven recordings, made in the middle and late 1920s after his return to Chicago.

The thirties found Satchmo (garbled from Satchelmouth) visiting Europe for the first time and fronting a big band in the United States. His unique, hoarse vocalizing was both parallel and adjunct to his trumpet playing. Appearances in films, such as *Pennies From Heaven* with Bing Crosby, added to his popularity.

After a featured part in the film *New Orleans* in 1947, Armstrong formed an all-star sextet. He appeared with groups of this size for the rest of his career, touring worldwide, often under the auspices of the State Department, and his recordings of *Mack the Knife* and *Hello Dolly* were quite successful. As illness began to hamper him in the late 1960s, Armstrong placed more emphasis on his singing and less on his playing. He died of heart trouble a few days after his seventy-first birthday. (*St. Louis Blues; Dippermouth Blues; Cake Walking Babies from Home; Struttin' with Some Barbecue; Big Butter and Egg Man from the West; Potato Head Blues; Hotter Than That; West End Blues; Weather Bird; Sweethearts on Parade; I Gotta Right to Sing the Blues*)

COUNT BASIE

(1904, Red Bank NJ–1985)
William Basie studied music with his mother, played piano as a child, and later studied organ informally with Fats Waller. Stranded while travelling with a vaudeville show in Kansas City, he played there briefly for silent movies before joining Walter Page's Blue Devils in 1928. In the thirties he played with Bennie Moten's orchestra, and after Moten died in 1935, Basie took many of the band's key personnel and formed his own group. Entrepreneur John Hammond heard it on the radio and helped to bring the band to New York. With some creative soloists, an "All-American" rhythm section, and several casual, "head" arrangements that were eventually made permanent, Basie became an international success.

His first band lasted until 1950, when economics forced him to scale down to a sextet for two years. In 1952 he reorganized a big band, this time with more formal arrangements. His recording of *Every Day*, with Joe Williams singing, helped the band to a new popularity. They went on to record with Frank Sinatra, Tony Bennett, Sarah Vaughan, and Billy Eckstine. After Basie's death the band carried on, with Thad Jones assuming the leadership in 1985.

As a pianist Basie was noted for a spare, humorous, encouraging style. In his later years he recorded often in small combinations with artists such as Dizzy Gillespie, Zoot Sims, and Oscar Peterson. (*Moten Swing; Doggin' Around; Taxi War Dance; Lester Leaps In; I Found a New Baby; Breakfast Feud*)

SIDNEY BECHET
(*1897, New Orleans–1959*)
At age six Bechet borrowed his brother's clarinet; about two years later he was sitting in with Freddie Keppard's band; during the next nine years, he played with all the important New Orleans jazzmen.

In 1919 Bechet joined Will Marion Cook's orchestra in New York and toured with him in Europe, staying behind to play in Paris and London until 1921. By the time he returned to the States, he had added soprano saxophone to his accomplishments, and his name became synonymous with that horn. Bechet had a pronounced vibrato, a sunny melodic style, and a driving attack that could play lead as strongly as a trumpet.

In the 1920s Bechet made a second trip to Europe, playing in Russia and again in Paris. In the early forties he had a hit with *Summertime* for the New York–based Blue Note label. Soon after World War II he moved to France and made his home there for his remaining years, revered as a popular entertainer and personality as well as a jazzman. (*Cake Walking Babies from Home; Blue Horizon*)

In a 1930s reunion, Sidney Bechet, Clarence Williams, and Louis Armstrong.
(Duncan Schiedt Collection)

BIX BEIDERBECKE

(1903, Davenport IA–1931)
Beiderbecke was, to many, the archetype of the heroic, ill-starred, self-destructive jazzman. Self-taught on piano and cornet and influenced on the latter by Emmett Hardy, Louis Armstrong, and Joe Smith, he forged a personal style that featured a subtle rhythmic sense and a burnished, mellow tone. Bix's piano was mainly a vehicle for presenting his compositions, such as *In a Mist, Candlelights,* and *In the Dark*—impressionist pieces that reflected his interest in Debussy and such American composers as Eastwood Lane.

Beiderbecke was the leading light in a group called the Wolverines in 1923. After working and jamming in Chicago, he joined Frankie Trumbauer's orchestra in St. Louis in 1926 and subsequently played with Trumbauer in the bands of Jean Goldkette and Paul Whiteman. Also with Trumbauer as well as on his own, he made a series of influential small group recordings in 1927–28.

After leaving Whiteman in 1930, Beiderbecke played with Glen Gray's orchestra in New York but died the following year of pneumonia complicated by alcoholism. (*Singin' the Blues; Riverboat Shuffle*)

CLIFFORD BROWN

(1930, Wilmington DE–1956)
At fifteen Brown took up the trumpet; subsequently he studied harmony, theory, and a variety of instruments privately; and at eighteen he began playing in Philadelphia with Charlie Parker, Miles Davis, and Fats Navarro. He was especially influenced stylistically and encouraged by Navarro.

After an automobile accident hospitalized him for a year in 1950–51, Brown became active again with Chris Powell's rhythm and blues group. In 1953 he played with Tadd Dameron's band and recorded with him and with his own quintet. Following a European tour with Lionel Hampton in the second half of the year, Brown free-lanced in New York with Art Blakey and others before joining Max Roach in California to form Brown–Roach Inc., a quintet that was soon among the best small groups in jazz. In June 1956 Brown was killed in an automobile accident on the Pennsylvania Turnpike. Numerous trumpeters, including Freddie Hubbard and Lee Morgan, were influenced by Brown's full-bodied sound and a delivery that was articulate at almost any tempo. (*Pent-Up House*)

DON BYAS

(1912, Muskogee OK–1972)
Don Byas worked with several important bands, including Don Redman's, Lucky Millinder's, and Andy Kirk's, before joining Count Basie's and recording his famous solo on *Harvard Blues* in 1941. In 1943 he played at clubs on New York's 52nd Street in a two-tenor group with Coleman Hawkins, one of his inspirations. Later Byas became involved with Dizzy Gillespie and the modern movement, wherein his sophisticated grasp of harmony enabled him to blend the new ideas with compatible elements in his own playing.

In 1946 he left for Europe with Redman's band and remained on the Continent playing and recording until 1970, when he returned to the States to play at the Newport Festival in New York and at clubs. In 1971 Byas toured Japan with Art Blakey before going back to Holland, where he died of lung cancer the following year. (*I Got Rhythm*)

BENNY CARTER

(b. 1907, New York City)
Mainly self-taught on a number of instruments, Carter went to Wilberforce University to study theology but left there with Horace Henderson's Wilberforce Collegians. He had a brief stint with Duke Ellington before working with Charlie Johnson's band at Smalls' Paradise in New York. After playing with Fletcher Henderson, Chick Webb, and McKinney's Cotton Pickers, Carter formed his own band in 1933.

He went to Paris in 1935, working there and later in England as a staff arranger for the BBC. In 1937 he led an interracial, international band at a Dutch seaside resort. Returning to the States in 1938, he re-formed his big band, which he led until 1941. Carter further established himself as a writer and instrumentalist of the top rank, with alto saxophone as his main instrument and trumpet as a strong double.

In the mid-1940s, another edition of his band that included Max Roach, Miles Davis, and J.J. Johnson was based in California, and Carter then began writing for films and, subsequently, television. In the 1970s he became active as a lecturer and conductor of college seminars and once again put forth his undiminished talents as an instrumentalist at festivals, concerts, and clubs throughout the world. (*I Can't Believe That You're in Love With Me; When Lights Are Low*)

CHARLIE CHRISTIAN
(*1916, Dallas–1942*)
After studying with his father and playing guitar in Oklahoma groups, Christian toured in Alphonso Trent's band and played with the Jeter-Pillars orchestra in St. Louis. When he joined the Benny Goodman Sextet in 1939, he opened up the world of electric guitar to countless players who were to follow in his footsteps. His linear, horn-like phrasing and urgent swing were the hallmarks of a style that was one of the bridges between swing and bop. Christian often sat in on the seminal sessions at Minton's Playhouse in Harlem during the time he was starring downtown in the Goodman Sextet. He died at twenty-six of tuberculosis. (*I Found a New Baby; Breakfast Feud*)

NAT "KING" COLE
(*1917, Montgomery AL–1965*)
While attending high school in Chicago, Cole worked in a band led by his brother, bassist Eddie Cole. He traveled to California with a revival of the musical *Shuffle Along* and, when it dis-

banded, remained in Los Angeles playing solo piano until he formed the King Cole Trio in 1937. The trio began recording in 1940 and made appearances on both coasts but did not gain much attention until the release of its Capitol recordings of 1943–46, beginning with *Straighten Up and Fly Right*. The piano-guitar-bass instrumentation spawned many trios in the same vein.

Cole's Earl Hines–derived, Art Tatum–influenced piano style was musically outstanding, but it was his mellow singing, on both jump tunes and ballads, that brought him his great popularity. By 1949 his recordings were predominantly vocals backed by large orchestras with strings—more pop than jazz. Although he maintained a quartet for night club jobs, Cole's pop work took precedence, and he became an international star. He died of lung cancer. (*Body and Soul,* third version)

ORNETTE COLEMAN
(*b. 1930, Fort Worth*)
Largely self-taught, Coleman began on alto saxophone at fourteen and played tenor with rhythm and blues groups in Texas before leaving for Los Angeles with Pee Wee Crayton's band. After gigging around he went back to Ft. Worth, then returned to Los Angeles in 1954. There he supported himself as an elevator operator and studied harmony and theory textbooks. He evolved a theory he subsequently called "harmolodics" in which his improvised melodies were not based on conventional chord progressions. His solo style sometimes sounded like a country blues singer with elements of a southwestern hoedown and essences of Charlie Parker. More than any other musician, Coleman influenced others, including Sonny Rollins and John Coltrane, to play in a free style.

In the summer of 1959 Coleman and his sidekick, trumpeter Don Cherry, attended the School of Jazz at Lenox, Massachusetts, and recorded for Atlantic before making their debut in a quartet at the Five Spot Cafe in New

John Coltrane in a favorite photograph.

York that fall. Among the subsequent albums for Atlantic was *Free Jazz,* thirty-seven minutes of spontaneous improvisation by a double quartet. In the mid-sixties he formed a trio with bassist David Izenzon and drummer Charles Moffett, touring Europe and recording in Scandinavia. In 1972 Coleman added saxophonist Dewey Redman to his quartet and combined it with a symphony orchestra to play his extended work *Skies of America* at the Newport Jazz Festival in New York. In the eighties Coleman's groups began using two guitars and electric bass, and his music more and more reflected his early rhythm-and-blues experience. (*Lonely Woman; Congeniality; Free Jazz*)

JOHN COLTRANE
(*1926, Hamlet NC–1967*)

Coltrane studied several instruments in high school, including the saxophone, and in the early 1950s attended music schools in Philadelphia. He worked there with a small group and in Hawaii with a Navy band in 1945–46. After experience with singer Eddie Vinson (1947–48), he played alto with Dizzy Gillespie's big band from 1949, switching to tenor in Gillespie's small group of 1950–51. Following stints with Earl Bostic and Johnny Hodges between 1952 and 1954, he joined Miles Davis's group for two years in 1955 and his personal style began to emerge. He gained important experience in 1957 with Thelonious Monk's quartet, free-lanced around New York with Red Garland and Donald Byrd, and played again with Davis on and off between 1958 and 1960. In 1960 he formed his own quartet with McCoy Tyner, Jimmy Garrison, and Elvin Jones. The group's numbers sometimes went on for an hour, with Coltrane, stoked by Jones, reaching emotional heights that put the audience into, alternately, a frenzy and a trance. On one of these pieces, a modal treatment of Richard Rodgers's *My Favorite Things*, he played soprano saxophone, an instrument he repopularized. On tenor he exerted a great influence on an army of young players.

In 1965 Coltrane's group changed in character when his second wife, the former Alice McLeod, replaced Tyner, drummer Rashied Ali at first played alongside Jones, and Pharoah Sanders joined on second reed, a role Eric Dolphy had once filled. Coltrane moved away from modal improvising and in the direction of free jazz in such compositions as *Ascension*. He died of a liver ailment in 1967. (*So What; Alabama*)

TADD DAMERON
(*1917, Cleveland OH–1965*)
Dameron studied music with his brother, Caesar, an alto saxophonist. He began playing piano professionally with trumpeter Freddie Webster, then played with the bands of Zack Whyte and Blanche Calloway. As an arranger he was active from 1940 with Vido Musso and in Kansas City with Harlan Leonard's Rockets. In New York in the forties, he wrote for Jimmie Lunceford, Georgie Auld, Sarah Vaughan, and Dizzy Gillespie and was one of the composers who helped bring bop to the big bands. From 1947 he led his own small groups featuring trumpeter Fats Navarro. After playing at the Paris Jazz Festival in 1949 with Miles Davis, Dameron went to England where he wrote for Ted Heath. A 1953 Dameron band that played in Atlantic City helped introduce Clifford Brown to the jazz public.

Following a long incarceration for a drug violation, Dameron returned to writing and arranging in 1961 with recordings under his own name and for others, including Benny Goodman. His best-known compositions include *Hot House, If You Could See Me Now, Foutainebleau, Lady Bird,* and *Our Delight*. Dameron died of cancer in 1965. (*Lady Bird*)

MILES DAVIS
(*b. 1926, Alton IL*)
The son of a dentist and prosperous farmer, Davis began playing trumpet at thirteen and worked with local bands. He was influenced early on by Clark Terry. After studying briefly at Juilliard, Davis played with the combos of Charlie Parker and Coleman Hawkins and the big bands of Benny Carter and Billy Eckstine. In 1947–48 he became part of Parker's quintet before forming his own history-making nonet in 1948–49.

In the mid-fifties Davis began leading a quintet (sometimes a sextet), that over the next thirteen years included such luminaries as John Coltrane, Red Garland, Cannonball Adderly, Paul Chambers, Philly Joe Jones, Hank Mobley, Wynton Kelly, Jimmy Cobb, Bill Evans, George Coleman, Herbie Hancock, Ron Carter, and Tony Williams. His collaborations with Gil Evans, begun in the nonet, continued in such albums as *Miles Ahead, Sketches of Spain,* and *Porgy and Bess,* each of which placed Davis in a large orchestral setting.

Davis's 1959 album, *Kind of Blue,* popularized modal improvisation in the 1960s, but in the early seventies he turned more to electronic music, utilizing synthesizers, amplifying his trumpet with a wa-wa pedal, and mixing elements of rock, funk, salsa, and modal jazz in such albums as *In A Silent Way, Bitches Brew,* and *Live-Evil,* which set the style for fusion and jazz rock. Doubling on synthesizer, he continued this style into the eighties. (*Klactoveedsedstene; Crazeology; Boplicity; Summertime; So What*)

ERIC DOLPHY
(*1928, Los Angeles–1964*)
Dolphy began studying clarinet in
1937. He worked with Roy Porter's big
band in the forties and Gerald Wilson,
Buddy Collette, and Eddie Beal in the
fifties, and gained wider exposure playing alto saxophone and flute with
Chico Hamilton's quintet in 1958–59.
In 1960 he established residence in
New York, started recording as a
leader, and played with Charles Mingus. He co-led a quintet with trumpeter Booker Little at the Five Spot in
1961 and in that same year toured and
recorded with John Coltrane. Dolphy
formed his own group with Freddie
Hubbard in 1962 and recorded with
Ornette Coleman in the LP *Free Jazz*.

In 1964 he rejoined Mingus for a
tour of Europe and remained on the
Continent to play and record in Scandinavia and Holland. He died that year
in Berlin, apparently of complications
from diabetes.

Dolphy was a dramatic player on all
three of his instruments. While with
Hamilton he showed the strong influence of Charlie Parker, but in New
York he developed his own style, an
oblique, sometimes dissonant approach that became particularly personal on bass clarinet. (*Free Jazz*)

ROY ELDRIDGE
(*b. 1911, Pittsburgh PA*)
Eldridge studied with his saxophonist
brother Joe, with whom he co-led a
small band in the 1930s. His early
playing experience included the bands
of Horace Henderson, Zack Whyte, and
Speed Webb in the Midwest.

Eldridge moved to New York in 1930
and worked with a variety of groups.
His trumpet was featured with Teddy
Hill's band in radio broadcasts that
influenced the young Dizzy Gillespie,
among many others. After playing with
Fletcher Henderson in 1936–37, Eldridge led his own group in Chicago.
In the forties his fame spread through
his playing and singing with Gene
Krupa's orchestra. He also was on staff
at CBS and worked with Artie Shaw. In
the fifties Eldridge began an association with "Jazz at the Philharmonic"
and in the sixties appeared often with
Coleman Hawkins in clubs and concerts. He also was with Count Basie
briefly in 1966. From 1970 he led the
band at Jimmy Ryan's Club in New
York until poor health forced him first
to limit himself to singing and then
into semi-retirement.

Eldridge's volatile, passionate style
kept him a vital player long after Gillespie had assumed the mantle of stylistic leader that Eldridge himself had
inherited from Louis Armstrong in the
late 1930s. (*You'd Be So Nice to Come
Home To; Rockin' Chair; I Can't Believe That You're in Love With Me*)

DUKE ELLINGTON
(*1899, Washington DC–1975*)
Edward Kennedy Ellington began
studying piano privately at seven and
continued his musical education during his teens by listening to local ragtime pianists. He also had taken up
commercial art but reputedly refused
an art scholarship to Pratt Institute in
order to pursue music. By 1918 he was
not only a Washington area bandleader
but an entrepreneur, furnishing bands
for various social functions around
town. In 1923 he moved to New York,
where he led his own group and wrote
for revues at the Kentucky Club. The
band moved to the Cotton Club in
1927 and remained there until 1931,
gradually achieving international recognition through film appearances,
radio broadcasts, recordings, and a
European tour.

Ellington's "jungle" period of the
late twenties, with its growling effects
in the brass, and his early masterpieces of 1930–33—*Old Man Blues,
Daybreak Express, Mood Indigo,* and
others—gave way to even more sophisticated compositions that continued to reveal his unique gifts as composer-orchestrator. About 1938 he
entered a particularly fertile period,
creating popular songs such as *I Got It
Bad,* instrumental gems such as *Dusk,
Harlem Air Shaft,* and *Conga Brava,*

and jazz standards such as *In a Mellotone* and *Perdido*. His extended works, which had begun with *Creole Rhapsody* in 1931, continued with *Reminiscing in Tempo* in 1935 and reached a plateau with *Black, Brown, and Beige* in 1943.

In the fifties Ellington wrote *Suite Thursday* for the Monterey Jazz Festival and the score for the film *Anatomy of a Murder*. In the sixties he began a series of "Sacred Concerts," which he continued to present in churches here and abroad into the seventies. He also wrote several suites during those two decades, including the *Far East Suite*. Though underrated as a pianist, Ellington has been widely celebrated as a composer for his ability to use his ensemble as his instrument, bringing hitherto unknown colors and textures from the jazz orchestra. By the time of his death, Ellington had heard himself called a major twentieth-century composer regardless of category or style. (*East St. Louis Toddle-Oo; The New East St. Louis Toodle-O; Diminuendo in Blue and Crescendo in Blue; Ko-Ko; Concerto for Cootie; Cotton Tail; In a Mellotone; Blue Serge*)

BILL EVANS
(*1929, Plainfield NJ–1980*)
A student of piano, violin, and flute, Evans had his own group with his brother at sixteen. After earning a degree from Southwestern Louisiana College, he played piano with Mundell Lowe, Red Mitchell, and Herbie Fields and then went into the army. Following his discharge in 1954 he played with Jerry Wald and Tony Scott, with whom he attracted the attention of the jazz inner circle. Recommended to Riverside records by his colleagues, he made his first album in 1956. He also recorded with George Russell before joining Miles Davis in February 1958. He left the Davis group in November, but not before he took part in the modally directed LP *Kind of Blue*. Evans then led his own trios until his death in 1980. His recorded collaborations included albums with Jim Hall,

Stan Getz, and singer Tony Bennett.

Evans evinced a romantic, introspective style on ballads and was able to retain this very personal harmonic approach while swinging with great intensity on medium and up-tempo pieces. (*So What; Blue in Green*)

ART FARMER
(*b. 1928, Council Bluffs IA*)
Born in Iowa and raised in Phoenix, Art Farmer moved to Los Angeles in his teens and was soon playing trumpet with a variety of bands. He freelanced in New York in 1947–48 before returning to Los Angeles and working with Benny Carter's band and Wardell Gray's group. After touring with Lionel Hampton in 1952–53, he settled in New York, playing and recording with Gigi Gryce, Horace Silver, and Gerry Mulligan. From 1959 to '62 Farmer co-led the Jazztet with tenor saxophonist and composer Benny Golson, then performed in a quartet with Jim Hall. During this period he gave up trumpet to concentrate on flugelhorn exclusively. In 1968 he moved to Vienna but continued to tour worldwide. He and Golson revived the Jazztet in the 1980s. (*Moon Rays*)

ELLA FITZGERALD
(*b. 1918, Newport News VA*)
Ella Fitzgerald first attracted attention in 1934 when she won first prize in an amateur contest at Harlem's Apollo Theatre. She soon joined Chick Webb's orchestra and remained with the band into 1940, leading it for a year following Webb's death in 1939. By the time of her 1940 hit, a swinging version of the nursery rhyme *A-Tisket, A-Tasket*, Ella was already renowned among other singers and players for her tone, range, rhythmic drive, and overall musicianship. Her reputation as a balladeer was confirmed in a Gershwin set she did with pianist Ellis Larkins in the early 1950s, and her wordless improvisations set standards for scat singing.

In 1946 Fitzgerald formed an association with Norman Granz, touring with

Erroll Garner. *(Duncan Schiedt Collection)*

"Jazz at the Philharmonic" and recording for his Verve label. Usually accompanied by her own trio, Fitzgerald has appeared in countless jazz festivals, television specials, and films. (*You'd Be So Nice to Come Home To*)

ERROLL GARNER
(1921, Pittsburgh–1977)
Born into a musical family—his father three sisters, and brother all played piano—Erroll Garner was a child prodigy who reputedly never learned to read music. He came to national prominence on New York's 52nd Street and through recordings in the mid-1940s with the Slam Stewart trio and with his own trio.

Garner's unique style, a guitar-like left-hand cushioning a delayed-action, single-note melodic right hand, reached out to audiences not usually oriented in jazz. His ballad approach was languorously romantic, whether he was playing a pop standard or his own most celebrated composition, *Misty*.

Although his main vehicle was his trio, Garner also appeared with symphony orchestras from the 1950s through the seventies. He was featured extensively on television and booked as a concert artist by the dance and classical impresario S. Hurok. Garner died from a lung ailment of almost two years' duration. (*Fantasy on Frankie and Johnny*)

99

STAN GETZ
(*b. 1927, Philadelphia*)
Getz grew up in New York where he studied bass, bassoon, and then saxophone. From age sixteen he played in the bands of Jack Teagarden, Stan Kenton, and Benny Goodman, among others. He moved to California in 1947 and joined Woody Herman's reorganized band that fall as one of the Lester Young–inspired "Four Brothers" of its saxophone section. Getz's solo on *Early Autumn* brought him popularity that was reinforced by a series of recordings he made after leaving Herman. He led his own groups from 1949 but lived in Copenhagen in the late fifties.

In the early sixties Getz revived his career by introducing the bossa nova to the U.S., through albums made with guitarist Charlie Byrd and Brazilian singers João and Astrud Gilberto. Although he is still renowned for his ballad interpretations, Getz, whose tone has matured over the years, is capable of other moods as well, as he has shown in his performances of material by Bud Powell, Chick Corea, and Wayne Shorter. (*Body and Soul,* third version)

DIZZY GILLESPIE
(*b. 1917, Cheraw SC*)
After learning several instruments from his amateur musician father, John Birks Gillespie took up trombone in his mid-teens, then trumpet, and studied harmony and theory at Laurinburg Institute in North Carolina. He moved to Philadelphia in 1935, where he worked with local bands before joining

Dizzy Gillespie playing his specially built trumpet.

Teddy Hill in 1937 and playing in England and France with him.

In the Cab Calloway band, with which he became associated in 1939, Gillespie began experimenting with a more sophisticated approach to harmony and moved away from the influence of Roy Eldridge. Through section-mate Mario Bauza, Gillespie developed his interest in Afro-Cuban rhythms, which became part of the personal expression he brought to full flower in the mid-forties.

After meeting and playing together in the Earl Hines and Billy Eckstine bands, Gillespie and Charlie Parker co-led a quintet that, through club and concert appearances and recordings—all in 1945—ushered in the new force that came to be called bebop. Following the breakup of the quintet in 1946, Gillespie reorganized his orchestra, which had been unsuccessful a year earlier, and led it until early 1950. He also put together a big band for a State Department tour in 1956 and kept it intact until 1958, but, except for that and other occasional special events, Gillespie has led small combos since 1950.

A personality as well as a master musician, Gillespie is known for such compositions as *Night in Tunisia, Bebop, Woody'n You, Manteca, Con Alma, Anthropology,* and *Shaw 'Nuff,* the latter two written in collaboration with Parker. (*When Lights Are Low; Shaw 'Nuff; I Can't Get Started*)

BENNY GOODMAN
(*1909, Chicago–1986*)
A knee-pants prodigy, Goodman studied the clarinet at Hull House in Chicago and then joined Ben Pollack's band in California as a teenager. After moving to New York in 1929 and becoming a busy free-lancer, he formed his own band in 1934. Using, chiefly, Fletcher Henderson's arrangements, the band exploded on the national consciousness in 1935, ushering in the swing era of big bands.

Goodman led an orchestra almost continuously until mid-1944, during which time he also featured small jazz units ranging from trio to septet. By hiring instrumentalists such as Teddy Wilson, Lionel Hampton, Charlie Christian, and Cootie Williams, Goodman broke the color line at the same time he was presenting great music, aided in no small way by his own brilliant playing. Hampton and two other important Goodman sideman, Gene Krupa and Harry James, went on to successfully lead their own big bands.

Since the 1940s Goodman's major activity was as a combo leader, but from time to time he put together big bands that played abroad and appeared on television specials and retrospective concerts. (*Dinah,* first version; *Body and Soul,* first version; *I Found a New Baby*)

DEXTER GORDON
(*b. 1923, Los Angeles*)
The son of a physician whose patients included Duke Ellington and Lionel Hampton, Gordon studied harmony, theory, and reeds, and left school at seventeen to play tenor saxophone with a local band, the Harlem Collegians. In 1940 he joined Lionel Hampton's band for a three-year stint. After working with Louis Armstrong's big band in 1944, he began to make a name playing and recording with Billy Eckstine. Gordon appeared on 52nd Street with Charlie Parker and then spent most of the late 1940s back in California, where his activities included tenor saxophone battles with Wardell Gray.

Gordon synthesized the work of Lester Young, Coleman Hawkins, and Charlie Parker into a viable bop tenor style, which had a direct effect on Sonny Rollins and John Coltrane. He moved to Copenhagen in 1962 and enjoyed great popularity there. He soon began to tour widely in Europe and Japan and visited the U.S. periodically. The success of these visits and a new recording contract enabled him to take up residence in the States in the 1970s while continuing to tour internationally. (*Bikini*)

STEPHANE GRAPPELLI
(*b. 1908, Paris*)
Violinist Grappelli (originally Grappelly) gained world fame in the Quintette of the Hot Club of France with Django Reinhardt in the years 1934–39. During World War II he lived and played in England with George Shearing and others. After the war he returned to Paris and played at Club St. Germain des Prés and various hotels.

In the 1970s and eighties Grappelli, who also plays piano, began to tour internationally, appearing at festivals all over the globe. The elegant swing of his violin has rekindled the interest of his older fans and captured many listeners from younger generations. (*Dinah,* second version)

LIONEL HAMPTON
(*b. 1909 or '13, Louisville KY*)
Raised in Birmingham and Chicago, Hampton started on drums with the *Chicago Defender* Newsboys' band. He received some instruction on marimba and xylophone there, and then picked up the vibraphone in the late 1920s while playing with Les Hite's band in California. He recorded on vibes and drums with Louis Armstrong in 1930, appeared in films with him and with the Hite band, and studied music at USC. After leading his own band, Hampton was hired by Benny Goodman in 1936 and became a mainstay, particularly in the quartet and sextet but occasionally filling in on drums in the big band. He also revealed an infectious two-finger piano style and rhythmic vocalizing in the course of many all-star recording sessions he led during this period.

In 1940 Hampton left Goodman to form his own big band, which after two years established itself with a hit recording of *Flying Home,* featuring Illinois Jacquet, and sustained itself with Hampton's combination of musicianship and showmanship. Over the years he has boasted such soloists as Dexter Gordon, Joe Newman, Arnett Cobb, Clifford Brown, and Art Farmer. Hampton has remained a vital vibraphonist, whether at a Goodman reunion or in front of his own band, a format to which he invariably returns. (*When Lights Are Low*)

COLEMAN HAWKINS
(*1904, St. Joseph MO–1969*)
As a child, Coleman Hawkins played piano, cello, and, from the age of nine, tenor saxophone. While still a teenager he went on the road with Mamie Smith's Jazz Hounds. He left the tour to free-lance in New York, where he joined Fletcher Henderson's orchestra in 1924. In his ten years with Henderson, Hawkins established himself as a major soloist and the major tenor saxophonist in jazz.

In 1934, he accepted an invitation to join Jack Hylton's band in England. After touring on the continent, playing and recording with a variety of bands and musicians, including Django Reinhardt and Benny Carter, Hawkins returned to the United States in 1939. He recorded *Body and Soul,* a popular success as well as a masterpiece recording, and reestablished himself as a pre-eminent soloist. Shortly thereafter he fronted his own big band until early 1941, when he went back to small groups, appearing often in the 52nd Street clubs. In 1944 he led the first bebop recording session, featuring trumpet and composing by Dizzy Gillespie. Hawkins, in continuing to hire younger musicians, identified himself with the modern movement, with such sidemen as Thelonious Monk, Fats Navarro, and Howard McGhee. In the 1940s he toured with Norman Granz's "Jazz at the Philharmonic" concerts. He continued to tour with Granz here and abroad into 1967, but was most frequently heard as leader of his own groups. (*The Stampede; Body and Soul,* second version; *The Man I Love; I Can't Believe That You're in Love with Me*)

FLETCHER HENDERSON
(*1897, Cuthbert, GA–1952*)
Henderson started out to be a chemist, but when he came to New York in 1920 to do postgraduate work at New York University, he worked as a part-time pianist for W.C. Handy, as a house pianist for Black Swan records, and as accompanist for Ethel Waters.

From 1923 Henderson led his own big band which played often at the Roseland Ballroom in New York and toured extensively. Through its ranks passed some of the most celebrated instrumentalists of early jazz, including Louis Armstrong, Benny Carter, Coleman Hawkins, clarinetist Buster Bailey, and trombonist Jimmy Harrison. The band's arrangements were written by Don Redman, Henderson, and his brother Horace, who often played piano while Fletcher conducted.

Henderson's band never achieved success to equal its musical excellence. It was through Benny Goodman's big band, to which he contributed such arrangements as *Sometimes I'm Happy, Blue Skies, King Porter Stomp, Down South Camp Meeting,* and *Wrappin' It Up,* that Henderson gained his greatest acclaim. He played piano with Goodman for a few months in 1939 but again led his own units in Chicago and California during the forties. In 1950 he led the band at Bop City in New York for *The Jazz Train,* a revue for which he had written the score.

In December 1950 Henderson was leading the band at Café Society when he suffered a stroke. He died two years later. (*The Stampede; Wrappin' It Up*)

EARL HINES
(*1903, Pittsburgh–1983*)
Born into a musical family, Hines studied piano from the age of nine. He planned for a concert career but began leading his own trio in clubs while still in high school. He broke into the music business full time in Chicago with singer Lois Deppe and the bands of Carroll Dickerson, Sammy Stewart, and Jimmie Noone. In 1927 he teamed up with Louis Armstrong, and the recordings he made with Armstrong's Hot Five established Hines as an innovative stylist. He was called the trumpet-style pianist because of his right-hand, single-note lines.

In 1928, on his twenty-fifth birthday, Hines debuted at the Grand Terrace in Chicago as leader of a big band which was also part of a large revue. He toured and recorded with various editions of this orchestra until 1948, when he disbanded to join Armstrong's all-star sextet.

From 1951 Hines worked with small groups in California, settling in San Francisco in 1956. A series of three concerts at New York's Little Theatre in 1964 catapulted him back into international recognition and activity. From that time until his death in 1983, he toured all over the world, including the Soviet Union in 1966. (*West End Blues; Weather Bird; Four or Five Times*)

BILLIE HOLIDAY
(*1915, Baltimore–1959*)
The daughter of Fletcher Henderson's sometime guitarist, Clarence Holiday, Billie moved to New York with her mother at age fourteen. She tried to find work as a dancer but wound up singing at Harlem clubs, where she was heard by John Hammond and Benny Goodman. She made her first recording with Goodman in 1933.

Through a series of records she made for Brunswick and Columbia with all-star combos (both her own and Teddy Wilson's) between 1935 and 1942, she gained an international reputation. She also sang for brief periods with the bands of Count Basie and Artie Shaw during this time.

In the forties and fifties Holiday appeared as a soloist in clubs and theaters. Her unique sound, her natural talent, and a pulsating phraseology derived largely from Louis Armstrong made her one of the great jazz singers. She was basically not a blues performer (although *Fine and Mellow* and *Billie's Blues* are among her most memorable performances) but rather an improvising stylist who elevated both superior and lame pop songs through her interpretations.

Her stormy life, marred by unhappy romantic alliances and narcotics addiction, ended in 1959. (*He's Funny That Way; These Foolish Things*)

MILT JACKSON
(*b. 1923, Detroit*)
Jackson studied music at Michigan State University and was playing in his home city when Dizzy Gillespie heard him and invited him to New York in 1945. After playing in the trumpeter's small band and orchestra, Jackson free-lanced with Howard McGhee, Tadd Dameron, and Thelonious Monk before replacing Terry Gibbs in Woody Herman's band in 1949. When he left Herman in 1950, he rejoined Gillespie's small group, playing vibraharp and piano until he left in 1952 to help form the Modern Jazz Quartet with John Lewis (q.v.).

During the first twenty-two years of the MJQ, Jackson occasionally led his own groups, often with his ex-Gillespie mate Ray Brown, and he continued to record as a leader.

In the 1940s Jackson emerged as the new force on vibraharp, rising to prominence in the fifties, a position he has maintained with his innate swing (even at the slowest tempos) and essential feel for the blues idiom. (*Misterioso; Evidence; Criss-Cross; Django*)

JAMES P. JOHNSON
(*1891, New Brunswick NJ–1955*)
Johnson studied piano with his mother and private teachers, and by the age of thirteen he was working professionally during summer vacations. First influenced by pianist Luckey Roberts, Johnson led small bands and played solo piano in various Harlem clubs and toured in vaudeville. He cut piano rolls for the Aeolian Company and made his first piano solo recordings in 1921. In the twenties Johnson also wrote theater music, including the score for the very successful *Runnin' Wild* (1923).

He was partially paralyzed by a stroke in 1940, and in 1951 another stroke rendered him speechless. He was bedridden until his death. Johnson's stride piano was a direct influence on Fats Waller and others. As a composer he is known for his piano pieces, like *Carolina Shout* and *Steeplechase (Over the Bars)*, and for such songs as *If I Could be With You One Hour Tonight, Old Fashioned Love*, and *Charleston*. (*Carolina Shout*)

SCOTT JOPLIN
(*1868, Texarkana TX–1917*)
The most celebrated of ragtime composers, Joplin worked as a piano soloist in bars and cabarets in St. Louis and Chicago, appearing at the Chicago World's Fair in 1893. Following the success of his *Maple Leaf Rag*, published in 1899, Joplin devoted himself to composing rather than playing. An alliance with music publisher John Stark brought forth such pieces as *The Entertainer, The Cascades*, and *Elite Syncopations*. Joplin's opera, *Treemonisha*, found no backers, and he published and staged it himself in 1911 in Harlem. His declining mental and physical condition during the next few years placed him in Manhattan State Hospital where he died in 1917. (*Maple Leaf Rag*, first version)

LEE KONITZ
(*b. 1927, Chicago*)
Konitz played with Chicago bands and was associated with pianist Lennie Tristano (q.v.), who became his teacher and mentor. After going on the road with the bands of Jerry Wald and Claude Thornhil, Konitz moved to New York and played with Tristano's groups and Miles Davis's nonet. Except for a year with Stan Kenton in 1952–53 and some brief reunions with Tristano, he has since led his own groups and taught extensively.

Of all the alto saxophonists who emerged in the time of Charlie Parker, Konitz is the most individual. He has absorbed the influences of Parker and Tristano yet remains an original and a

The Modern Jazz Quartet in the 1950s: from left, Percy Heath, Connie Kay, John Lewis, and Milt Jackson. (Frank Driggs Collection)

true improviser. His sound and style, often thought of as cool in the forties and fifties, have darkened and toughened as he has matured. (*Boplicity; Subconscious Lee*)

GENE KRUPA
(*1909, Chicago–1973*)
Krupa was at first influenced, along with many other young white Chicago musicians, by the black New Orleans jazzmen who migrated north in the 1920s. Later, like most drummers, he learned from Chick Webb's big band style. In 1927 he recorded with the McKenzie-Condon Chicagoans and two years later came to New York with Red McKenzie. In 1934 he joined Benny Goodman's orchestra where his feature on *Sing, Sing, Sing* brought him a popularity symbolic of the swing era itself and focused attention on drummers as never before.

In 1938 Krupa started his own band

and led it almost continuously until 1951. From that point on he led trios and quartets featuring various saxophonists. He also toured with "Jazz at the Philharmonic" and reunited with Goodman for special concerts and tv shows. Krupa died of leukemia in 1973. (*Dinah*, first version; *Body and Soul*, first version; *Rockin' Chair*)

JOHN LEWIS
(*b. 1920, La Grange IL*)
Raised in Albuquerque, John Lewis studied piano as a child, and at the University of New Mexico he divided his time between music and anthropology. In the army during World War II he met drummer Kenny Clarke who, in 1946, introduced him to Dizzy Gillespie. Gillespie commissioned Lewis to write for his orchestra and then hired him as his pianist.

After leaving Gillespie, Lewis worked with Illinois Jacquet, Charlie Parker,

Miles Davis's nonet, Lester Young, and others. In 1952 Lewis, who holds two degrees from the Manhattan School of Music, formed the Modern Jazz Quartet with Milt Jackson (q.v.), Percy Heath, and Kenny Clarke. With one change (Connie Kay replaced Clarke in 1955), the group stayed together until 1974, setting standards of excellence through their use of polyphony and their feeling for the blues idiom. The MJQ's repertoire included Lewis's compositions, Jackson's blues pieces, interpretations of jazz ballad standards, and jazz originals by Monk, Parker, and Gillespie.

In 1981 they reorganized for a tour of Japan and decided to continue performing together, first for at least three months of the year and later for longer stretches. Lewis has also remained active as a teacher and as a recording artist in his own right. (*Parker's Mood; Boplicity; Django*)

MEADE "LUX" LEWIS

(*1905, Chicago–1964*)
Although he had studied violin, Lewis was inspired to take up the piano when he heard bluesman Jimmy Yancey in Chicago. He began playing clubs and made his first of several recordings of the piece most closely associated with him, *Honky Tonk Train Blues*, in 1929.

He spent several years in obscurity until John Hammond found him washing cars in a Chicago garage in 1935 and brought him to New York. Together with Albert Ammons and Pete Johnson, Lewis led a boogie woogie revival with appearances at Café Society in New York and the 1938 *Spirituals to Swing* concert at Carnegie Hall.

In the 1940s Lewis moved to Los Angeles and continued playing there and on tour. He died as a result of an automobile accident. (*Honky Tonk Train Blues*)

JIMMIE LUNCEFORD

(*1902, Fulton MO–1947*)
Lunceford studied music in Denver under Paul Whiteman's father and later in Nashville at Fisk University. He became proficient on all the reeds, playing with the bands of Elmer Snowden and Wilbur Sweatman.

He taught high school music in Memphis and started his own band made up of his students. By the early 1930s it had begun to make its reputation, and from 1934, when Lunceford became associated with the Decca label, until 1942, the group's precise execution of difficult arrangements (mostly by Sy Oliver), its showmanship, and its two-beat swing made it one of the top bands in the world. Lunceford did not play but conducted with a baton.

On Lunceford's death, while the ensemble was on the road in Oregon in 1947, the leadership was assumed by saxophonist Joe Thomas and pianist Eddie Wilcox, but the band's peak had passed. (*Organ Grinder's Swing*)

CHARLES MINGUS

(*1922, Nogales AZ–1979*)
Mingus grew up in the Watts section of Los Angeles. He began on trombone, switched to cello, and at sixteen studied bass with Red Callender. He played in California with Buddy Collette, Louis Armstrong, and Barney Bigard and in 1947–48 with Lionel Hampton. He became more widely known with the Red Norvo Trio, with whom he traveled to New York in 1951. Settling there, Mingus played with Billy Taylor, Charlie Parker, Stan Getz, Duke Ellington, Bud Powell, and Art Tatum. He then started his own recording company, Debut, and formed his own group, the Jazz Workshop.

As a composer he was influenced by Ellington, Parker, black church music, modern classical music, and the blues. As a bassist, he was an outstanding soloist and ensemble player.

An outspoken, controversial figure, Mingus wrote an autobiographical work, *Beneath the Underdog*, published in 1971. (*Haitian Fight Song*)

MODERN JAZZ QUARTET
see JOHN LEWIS and MILT JACKSON

THELONIOUS MONK
(*ca. 1920, Rocky Mount NC–1982*)
Monk studied piano privately from an early age, played the organ in church, and traveled with a woman evangelist and faith healer before he was seventeen. He took part in the seminal 1940s sessions in Harlem that led to the development of modern jazz, and thus, along with Dizzy Gillespie, Charlie Parker, Oscar Pettiford, and Kenny Clarke, he was an early contributor to the movement. Except for brief stays with Lucky Millinder, Gillespie, and Coleman Hawkins, he led his own groups from the mid-forties on.

As a pianist Monk had his antecedents in the stride players of the Harlem school and in Teddy Wilson, but his spare style and his very personal rhythmic sense marked him as a soloist unlike anyone else. His composing was shaped by this same angularity, and his perfectly structured melodies won him the acceptance of some of his peers but, until the mid-1950s, not the critics or the jazz public.

Monk led his own quartet from 1960 into the early seventies and toured with the all-star group Giants of Jazz (Gillespie, Sonny Stitt, Art Blakey, et al) in 1971 and '72. An appearance at the Newport Jazz Festival–New York with his quartet in 1975 proved to be Monk's farewell, and because of illness he played no more in public. (*Misterioso; Evidence; Criss-Cross; I Should Care; Bag's Groove*)

WES MONTGOMERY
(*1925, Indianapolis–1968*)
As a teenager Montgomery taught himself to play guitar after hearing Charlie Christian on records and was playing professionally six months later. In 1948–50 he played with Lionel Hampton's orchestra but then returned home to Indianapolis where he led his own trio. In the late 1950s he worked and recorded with a San Francisco–based group, the Mastersounds, which included his brothers, Monk and Buddy, and later evolved into the Montgomery Brothers.

Montgomery's powerfully swinging, sometimes double-octave, style contrasted effectively with his swift, single-string work, which was thumbed rather than picked. He headed his own recording groups from 1959 on, and in 1965–66 he allied himself with the Wynton Kelly trio for clubs and records. The most influential guitarist after Charlie Christian, Montgomery expanded his audience when he began recording more subdued versions of popular songs like *Goin' Out of My Head* and *A Day in the Life* with orchestral accompaniment in 1965. He died of a heart attack at the height of his public success. (*West Coast Blues*)

JELLY ROLL MORTON
(*1890, New Orleans–1941*)
Morton (born Ferdinand Joseph Lamonthe or La Menthe) began his musical studies on guitar at age seven. Three years later he took up the piano and while still in his teens was reputedly a working "professor" in the bordellos of New Orleans's Storyville district. Dividing his time between music and other pursuits, Morton played in such cities as Memphis, St. Louis, and Kansas City and, in the years 1917–22, spent much time in California. A series of recordings, done mostly in Chicago and New York between 1926 and 1930 under the name Morton's Red Hot Peppers, established him as a composer and leader, but by 1937 he was in decline, hidden away in a small club in Washington, D.C. He recorded his reminiscences, his theory of jazz, and his piano and voice on a remarkable series of discs for the Library of Congress in 1938. In 1940 he returned to California where he died the following year. (*Maple Leaf Rag*, second version; *Black Bottom Stomp; Dead Man Blues; Grandpa's Spells; King Porter Stomp*)

BENNIE MOTEN
(1894, Kansas City MO–1935)
This Kansas City bandleader led his own orchestra from 1922 until his death following a tonsillectomy. By the late 1930s his sidemen, who helped fashion a style that typified southwestern swing, included Oran "Hot Lips" Page, Eddie Durham, Eddie Barefield, Jack Washington, Buster Smith, Ben Webster, Walter Page, Count Basie, and singer Jimmy Rushing. After Moten's death several of these players, under Basie's leadership, formed what became one of the most enduring organizations in jazz. (*Moten Swing*)

FATS NAVARRO
(b. 1923, Key West–1950)
Theodore Navarro first played tenor saxophone, then trumpet. In 1941–42 he played in Snookum Russell's band along with J.J. Johnson and Ray Brown. He was with Andy Kirk in 1943–44 before taking over Dizzy Gillespie's chair in the orchestra of singer Billy Eckstine and emerging as one of the brightest young disciples of the Gillespie-Parker movement.

Navarro's brilliant trumpet showed to its best advantage with Tadd Dameron's combo in 1947–48, but narcotics addiction ruined his health and he contracted the tuberculosis that resulted in his death. Navarro recorded as a leader as well as with Eckstine, Dameron, Illinois Jacquet, and Benny Goodman. His style had a direct effect on that of Clifford Brown. (*Lady Bird*)

JIMMY NOONE
(1895, Cut-off LA–1944)
Though he was two years older than Sidney Bechet, Noone studied with him after taking up the clarinet in 1905 and later replaced Bechet in Freddie Keppard's band. After working around New Orleans, Noone moved to Chicago in 1918 and studied there with Franz Schoepp, recorded for Gennett in 1923, and headlined quite successfully at the Apex Club in 1927 with Earl Hines as his pianist.

Noone, who undoubtedly influenced the young Benny Goodman and others, was known for his recordings of *I Know That You Know, Sweet Sue, Four Or Five Times, Apex Blues,* and, most particularly, *Sweet Lorraine.*

In the early 1940s he moved to Los Angeles and was featured with Kid Ory's band on radio and record dates. He also continued leading his own band until his sudden death from a heart attack. (*Four or Five Times*)

RED NORVO
(b. 1908, Beardstown IL)
Norvo (real name, Kenneth Norville) studied piano at age eight and then took up xylophone in high school. At seventeen he left home for Chicago, where he led his own groups (the first was a marimba band) as a solo act in vaudeville, and played with the orchestras of Paul Ash and Paul Whiteman. While with Whiteman he met singer Mildred Bailey, whom he married. She sang with the twelve-piece band they co-led in the late 1930s, and they became known as Mr. and Mrs. Swing. From 1940 to 1944 Norvo continued to lead his band, but Bailey worked on her own. (They were divorced in 1945.)

Norvo switched to vibraphone in 1943 and played the instrument xylophone style, with the electric vibrators turned off. After disbanding his ensemble in 1944, he worked with Benny Goodman (1945) and Woody Herman (1945–46). He also led a historic recording session in early 1945 with Charlie Parker, Dizzy Gillespie, Teddy Wilson, and Flip Phillips. In 1950 he led a trio with Tal Farlow and Charles Mingus that set a standard for small ensemble jazz.

Norvo, the first musician to adapt the xylophone to jazz, has spanned several stylistic eras. Despite hearing problems which caused a temporary retirement in the early 1970s, he has carried on with his own groups and as part of all-star tours and concerts, still a compelling performer. (*Body and Soul,* third version)

CHARLIE PARKER
(1920, Kansas City KS–1955)
Parker grew up on the Missouri side of the river, where he began studying alto saxophone in 1931. He tested his abilities, not too successfully at first, at local jam sessions, but his style matured during a season at a summer resort with George E. Lee's band in 1937. Parker gained his first recognition among musicians outside his area through recordings he made with Jay McShann's orchestra in 1941. After he left McShann in New York, he added harmonic sophistication to his already hard-swinging, blues-infused style and, in sessions at various Harlem clubs, developed into the soloist that helped change the language of jazz.

After playing in the Earl Hines and Billy Eckstine bands, Parker appeared on 52nd Street in a quintet he co-led with Dizzy Gillespie. The recordings he made with Gillespie and with his own group during this period had a profound and lasting effect on an entire generation of musicians. After recovering from a breakdown in 1946 in California, Parker returned to New York to form an outstanding and influential quintet with Miles Davis, Duke Jordan, Tommy Potter, and Max Roach. He continued to lead a quintet into the early fifties but also recorded and toured with a very popular ensemble that included a string section, in renditions of ballad standards. In the next few years Parker toured intermittently, often backed by pickup rhythm sections. He died in 1955 of physical ailments complicated by periods of narcotics addiction and alcoholism. (*Shaw 'Nuff; Lady Be Good; KoKo; Embraceable You* (both takes); *Klactoveedsedstene; Parker's Mood; Crazeology*)

BUD POWELL
(1924, New York–1966)
Earl "Bud" Powell came from a musical family. He won prizes for Bach recitals as a schoolboy but, by his mid-teens, was playing piano with bands around the city, including Valaida Snow's. Encouraged by Thelonious Monk, Powell sat in at the Harlem sessions that gave birth to bebop. When that music moved downtown, he became part of the 52nd Street club scene and took part in many recording sessions for Savoy records, including his extended solos on *Webb City* and *Fat Boy* with the Bebop Boys. His harmonic acuity and relentless attack established him as a kind of pianistic counterpart of Charlie Parker.

Although hampered by mental illness, Powell managed, through his recordings and trio performances, to exert a major influence on jazz. In 1959 he moved to France, received artistic recognition, and recaptured much of his power. He was slowed by tuberculosis in 1962 but returned again to performances after a convalescence. Powell returned to the States in 1964, played erratically, and died after a lingering illness. (*Night in Tunisia*)

DON REDMAN
(1900, Piedmont WV–1964)
This diminutive jazz giant was a child prodigy who played trumpet at three and, during his childhood, studied every instrument in the band as well as harmony, theory, and composition. Conservatory-trained in Boston and Detroit, Redman joined Fletcher Henderson in 1923 and remained with the band for three years. From 1927 to '31 he was musical director of McKinney's Cotton Pickers. He then led his own orchestra from 1931 to '40, and it became the first black band to play a sponsored radio series. In the forties Redman wrote for Paul Whiteman, Jimmy Dorsey, Count Basie, and others. He also led a big band for occasional night club and recording work and, in 1946–47, for a European tour. In the fifties and sixties he served as musical director for Pearl Bailey.

Redman's main instrument was alto sax; he also played tenor and baritone saxes and sang in a quasi-conversational style. His arrangements, for the Henderson band particularly, set the basic style for big band swing. (*The Stampede*)

DJANGO REINHARDT

(*b. 1910, Liverchies, Belgium–1953*)
Jean Baptiste Reinhardt spent his youth travelling through Belgium and France with his family in their gypsy caravan, learning to play violin, banjo, and guitar. When he was eighteen his left hand was severely burned in a fire, and he lost the use of two fingers. He overcame this handicap to become one of jazz's most original guitarists. In 1934 he and violinist Stephane Grappelli joined forces in the Quintette of the Hot Club of France and established an international reputation during the next five years through recordings. Reinhardt also recorded with visiting American musicians, including Coleman Hawkins, Benny Carter, and Dicky Wells.

Reinhardt visited the United States only once, touring with Duke Ellington just after World War II, but he was the first foreign musician to exert a major influence on American jazzmen. He is still highly regarded today for his passionate, romantic playing, which continues to influence young musicians. (*Dinah,* second version)

MAX ROACH

(*b. 1925, probably North Carolina*)
Roach grew up in Brooklyn and worked at Monroe's Uptown House in Harlem with Charlie Parker in 1942. Influenced by Kenny Clark, he developed his own style and became the premier drummer in the bop movement, grasping and complementing its rhythmic nuances to perfection. He recorded with Coleman Hawkins in 1944 and played with Benny Carter's orchestra and with Dizzy Gillespie on 52nd Street the following year. From 1947–49 he was with Charlie Parker's landmark quintet. In the fifties he was a regular at the Lighthouse in Hermosa Beach, California, before forming a group with Clifford Brown. That quintet set standards of excellence in the middle fifties, at the height of the "hard bop" period. Roach has continued to lead his own combos and has

formed a percussion ensemble, M'Boom, for recordings and concerts. He also appears as a solo performer, and in 1972 he joined the music faculty at the University of Massachusetts. (*KoKo; Embraceable You* (both takes); *Klacktoveedsedstene; Parker's Mood; Crazeology; Night in Tunisia; Blue 7; Pent-Up House*)

SONNY ROLLINS

(*b. 1929, New York City*)
Theodore Walter Rollins took up the saxophone in high school and played in a neighborhood band with saxophonist Jackie McLean, pianists Kenny Drew and Walter Bishop, and drummer Arthur Taylor, among others. By 1947 Rollins had switched from alto to tenor, and in 1948 he recorded with Babs Gonzales. Other recordings soon followed with J.J. Johnson, Bud Powell, and in 1951 with Miles Davis, who encouraged him and helped foster his career.

In the mid-1950s Rollins spent some time in Chicago, and left there as a member of the Max Roach–Clifford Brown quintet in 1956. The following year he formed his own group and has headed his own combos ever since, occasionally withdrawing from the working arena for self-contemplation and practice (in 1959–61 and again in 1968–71).

Rollins's full-bodied saxophone, at first shaped by Lester Young, Ben Webster, Dexter Gordon, and Charlie Parker, evolved into one of the most personal in jazz, displaying an architechtonic sense of structure and a sophisticated rhythmic variety. (*Pent-Up House; Blue 7*)

HORACE SILVER

(*b. 1928, Norwalk CT*)
Silver studied saxophone in high school and piano with a church organist. He worked local jobs on both instruments but was playing piano when Stan Getz heard him in Hartford and hired him for his quintet. He played with Getz in 1950–51 and then worked

Clifford Brown and Sonny Rollins in 1956. *(Photo by Charles Stewart)*

with Art Blakey, Terry Gibbs, Coleman Hawkins, Oscar Pettiford, and Lester Young during the next several years. As both pianist and chief composer, he was a charter member of the group with Blakey, Kenny Dorham, Hank Mobley, and Doug Watkins that became the Jazz Messengers. In 1956 Silver began leading his own quintet. In the forefront of the reaction to cool jazz in the mid-1950s, Silver combined elements of bebop with a bluesy, gospel-inspired approach which was often described with the adjective *funky*. (*Moon Rays*)

BESSIE SMITH

(*1894 or '95, Chattanooga TN–1937*) "The Empress of the Blues" began working with travelling shows in 1912 and soon became a featured performer, appearing from Atlantic City to Oklahoma and frequently leading her own revues. In 1923, following an unsuccessful audition at Okeh Records (where her voice was described as "too rough"), Smith recorded *Downhearted Blues* for Columbia, accompanied by pianist Clarence Williams and a small group. Within a year, her recordings had sold more than two million copies. Between 1924 and 1927 she recorded in the company of Louis Armstrong, Joe Smith, Don Redman, James P. Johnson, and Fletcher Henderson and was a headliner on the black vaudeville circuit.

By the late 1920s Smith's career had declined, although she continued to tour in vaudeville and was featured in the short film *St. Louis Blues*. In 1933 she recorded her last session for Columbia. She died in an automobile accident. (*St. Louis Blues; Lost Your Head Blues*)

ART TATUM

(*1910, Toledo OH–1956*) Blind in one eye and with only minimal vision in the other, Tatum studied violin at thirteen but soon took up the piano and gained early experience playing at local radio stations and clubs.

In 1932 he came to New York as singer Adelaide Hall's accompanist, and was soon receiving recognition for his virtuoso solo performances at the Onyx Club. He then led his own band at the Three Deuces in Chicago and in 1938 played in London.

Following many years as a solo pianist, Tatum formed a trio in 1943 with guitarist Tiny Grimes and bassist Slam Stewart that was to be his most successful format with the public. In his last few years he made an extensive series of solo recordings that spotlighted his speed and delicacy of touch, the swift interaction between his hands, and his prodigious harmonic imagination. Tatum died of uremia in 1956. (*Willow Weep for Me; Too Marvelous for Words*)

CECIL TAYLOR

(*b. 1933, New York City*) Taylor studied piano privately as well as at the New York College of Music and, for four years, at the New England Conservatory. His quartet in the mid-1950s (with Steve Lacy, Buell Neidlinger, and Dennis Charles) announced the pianist as a herald of the avant garde, although he was still using such pieces as *Sweet and Lovely* and Billy Strayhorn's *Johnny Come Lately* as his points of departure. Taylor continued to lead his own groups which, from the 1960s, most often included alto saxophonist Jimmy Lyons and drummer Andrew Cyrille. Taylor's intensely textural and percussive playing was much influenced by modern classical music, most particularly that of Stravinsky, Bartok, and Messiaen. He exhibits incredible energy rather than conventional swing, and jagged layers of sound rather than legato lines. In addition to appearances with his groups, Taylor has also performed in tandem with Max Roach, in a joint concert with Mary Lou Williams, and as a solo pianist. (*Enter Evening*)

*A Lennie Tristano group
in rehearsal: from left,
Lee Konitz, Warne Marsh,
Tristano, Billy Bauer,
and Jeff Morton.*
*(Photo by Herman Leonard,
courtesy of Charles Stewart)*

JACK TEAGARDEN
(*b. 1905, Vernon TX–1964*)
Virtually self-taught, Teagarden began on trombone at seven. He played with pianist Peck Kelley's band in 1921–23, then with Doc Ross until coming to New York in 1927. There, he played with Ben Pollack's orchestra (1928–33) and Paul Whiteman (1933–38). Teagarden led his own band from 1939 to 1946 and joined Louis Armstrong's all-stars in 1947, with whom he remained until the end of 1951. He organized his own combo and toured with it until he died of bronchial pneumonia in New Orleans in 1964.

Teagarden, who set standards for his trombone contemporaries, combined a technical expertise—range, facility, and tone—with a blues sensibility and relaxed swing. His singing, whether solo or in duets with Armstrong, exhibited some of the same warmth and style. (*Dinah,* first version)

LENNIE TRISTANO
(*1919, Chicago–1978*)
Suffering from influenza-weakened eyesight as an infant, Tristano was totally blind by age nine. He became proficient on reed instruments but concentrated on piano, playing in clubs, teaching, and developing his own harmonic language during the first half of the 1940s. Encouraged by bassist Chubby Jackson, he moved to New York where he led his own trio before forming a sextet that included saxophonists Lee Konitz and Warne Marsh. The sonority and dynamics of the group influenced the cool jazz of the 1950s, and their *Intuition* was the first recorded example of free, collective improvisation in jazz.

Tristano opened his own school in 1951 and thereafter devoted himself mostly to teaching. In 1958–59 he worked at the Half Note after a long period of no public performances. In the sixties he played occasionally at the Half Note and in Leeds, England. (*Subconscious Lee*)

FRANKIE TRUMBAUER
(*1901, Carbondale IL–1956*)
Trumbauer, whose name is synonymous with the C-melody saxophone, was closely associated with Bix Beiderbecke during the 1920s, both in his own band and with Jean Goldkette's and Paul Whiteman's orchestras. In 1927–28 Trumbauer and Beiderbecke made a series of important small band recordings under their own names. Lester Young cited Trumbauer's solo on *Singin' the Blues* as having greatly influenced him.

Trumbauer was raised in St. Louis and led his own band there before and after his years with Whiteman. A licensed pilot, he became active with the Civil Aeronautics Authority in 1940 and was a test pilot throughout World War II. From 1945–47 he played with Russ Case's studio group and Raymond Paige's NBC orchestra. (*Singin' the Blues; Riverboat Shuffle*)

SARAH VAUGHAN
(*b. 1924, Newark NJ*)
Beginning at age seven Vaughan sang in church and for eight years took piano lessons. She joined Earl Hines's band as vocalist and second pianist in 1943 and then sang with the Billy Eckstine band in 1944–45 and the John Kirby Sextet briefly in 1945–46. From the time of her first recordings with small groups in the mid-forties, some of them with Charlie Parker and Dizzy Gillespie, she revealed a facility for the harmonic language of the beboppers. Her rich contralto voice, with its warmth and great range, and a developing array of vocal techniques placed her in the front rank of contemporary singers, a position she maintained into the 1980s. Since the 1950s she has for the most part appeared with her own trio, but she also performs with larger orchestral backing including symphonic ensembles. (*All Alone; My Funny Valentine*)

Fats Waller in 1931. *(Duncan Schiedt Collection)*

FATS WALLER

(1904, New York City–1943)
After intensive study Thomas Waller, the son of a clergyman, became a professional pianist at fifteen. During the 1920s he played in cabarets, accompanied blues singers, and played organ in silent movie houses.

In 1934 Fats Waller and His Rhythm (his sextet) began recording Waller compositions and humorous treatments of popular songs for Victor. In his solo recordings, he elaborated on the stride style of his mentor, James P. Johnson.

Waller is remembered as a comical entertainer but also as an instrumentalist of commanding swing and a composer of some exceptional piano pieces and several durable popular songs.

At the time of his death, aboard a transcontinental train in Kansas City, Waller was a popular figure, having appeared in *Stormy Weather* and several other feature films. (*I Ain't Got Nobody*)

DICKY WELLS

(*1909, Centerville TN–1985*)
Raised in Louisville, Wells came to
New York in 1926 and played with several bands before touring with the
Benny Carter and Fletcher Henderson
orchestras in 1932–34. After a substan-
tial stay with Teddy Hill, he joined
Count Basie where he gained his
greatest recognition between 1938 and
'46. Wells's sly, leaping, slurring style
was heard to advantage in many of the
big band's numbers and also in the
small group recording *Dicky's Dream.*

Wells toured with Ray Charles's
band in the early sixties, but much of
his work in the post-Basie years was
with his ex-Basie mates Buck Clayton,
Buddy Tate, and Earle Warren. (*Taxi
War Dance*)

TEDDY WILSON

(*1912, Austin TX–1986*)
Educated in music at Tuskegee Institute and Talladega College, Wilson
moved to Detroit in 1929 and played
with local bands there and in Toledo
before landing in Chicago two years
later. After gaining valuable experience
with Erskine Tate, Louis Armstrong,
and Jimmie Noone, he moved to New
York in 1933, where he joined Benny
Carter and recorded with the Chocolate Dandies.

In 1934–35 Wilson played with Willie
Bryant's band and accompanied the
Charioteers. Then in July of the later
year he made history, breaking the
color line when he joined Benny
Goodman's trio. Wilson stayed with
Goodman, playing with the small units
and occasionally the big band, into
1939. After leading his own short-lived
big band, Wilson headed a sextet at
Cafés Society Uptown and Downtown
from 1940 to '44. Between 1936 and
1942 he also participated in the historic recordings with Billie Holiday.

In the forties and fifties Wilson
taught at Juilliard, was on staff at
WNEW radio and CBS television, and
made concert appearances here and
abroad. After portraying himself in *The
Benny Goodman Story* in 1956, he
began playing clubs with his own trio.

116

The trio remained his main format
into the 1980s, although he also
worked frequently as a solo pianist.

Wilson, who drew from Hines,
Tatum, and Waller, was noted for his
symmetrically swinging, single-note
right-hand lines, spun in an easy, understated, melodic style. He was a
major pianist and a major influence,
particularly during the late 1930s and
early forties. (*I Gotta Right to Sing the
Blues; Body and Soul,* first version)

WORLD SAXOPHONE QUARTET:
   HAMIET BLUIETT (*b. 1940,
      Lovejoy IL*);
   JULIUS HEMPHILL (*b. 1940,
      Ft. Worth TX*);
   OLIVER LAKE (*b. 1944,
      Marianna AR*);
   DAVID MURRAY (*b. 1955,
      Berkeley CA*)

This multi-reed group played its first
engagement at a Southern University
concert in New Orleans in December
1976, but it was not named the World
Saxophone Quartet until a 1977 appearance at the Tin Palace in New
York. The quartet draws on the free
jazz of Ornette Coleman for its solos
and collective improvisation, and on
Bartok and Ellington for some of its
writing, alternating between the improvised and the written for disciplined
contrast.

The basic instrumentation of the
WSQ is Lake and Hemphill, alto saxo-
phones; Murray, tenor saxophone;
Bluiett, baritone saxophone. Flutes and
clarinets are sometimes used, with
Murray also doubling on bass clarinet.

Hemphill, Lake, and Bluiett were
associated in St. Louis with the Black
Artists' Group, a musical collective
formed along the lines of Chicago's
Association for the Advancement of
Creative Musicians. The three, along
with Murray, became active in New
York avant garde circles during the
1970s. Each member of the quartet
maintains a separate musical life of his
own, and in the eighties Murray led
small groups in New York clubs as
well as a large ensemble. (*Steppin'*)

Lester Young. *(Photo by Charles Stewart)*

LESTER YOUNG

(1909, Woodville MS–1959)
From 1919 to 1928, Lester Young
played in the family band led by his
father, William "Billy" Young. He began
on drums but took up saxophone at
thirteen when the band was based in
Minneapolis.

Young worked with King Oliver and
Bennie Moten before joining Count
Basie in 1934. After a brief stint with
Fletcher Henderson, during which he
was unfavorably and unfairly compared with his predecessor Coleman
Hawkins, Young rejoined Basie in 1936
and helped change the course of jazz
with his almost vibrato-less sound, legato phrasing, and rhythmic originality
on the tenor saxophone. He also
showed a unique talent and personality on the clarinet on the few occasions he played it.

After an unfortunate Army experience, Young resumed his career as a
combo leader. Other than tours as a
soloist with "Jazz at the Philharmonic,"
this was his setting until his death in
1959.

During his Basie years Young participated in many of the Billie Holiday–
Teddy Wilson recordings, his lyrical
swing complementing Holiday's singing
to perfection. He nicknamed her Lady
Day and she called him Prez, short for
President. (*He's Funny that Way; Doggin' Around; Taxi War Dance; Lester
Leaps In*)

—*Ira Gitler*

Suggestions for Further Reading

Allen, Walter C. *Hendersonia: The Music of Fletcher Henderson.* Highland Park, New Jersey: privately published, 1973.
Armstrong, Louis. *Satchmo: My Life in New Orleans.* New York: Prentice Hall, 1954.

Balliett, Whitney. *American Musicians: 56 Portraits in Jazz.* New York: Oxford University Press, 1986.
____. *New York Notes.* New York: Da Capo Press, 1977.
____. *The Sound of Surprise.* New York: Dutton, 1959.
____. *Such Sweet Thunder.* Indianapolis: Bobbs-Merrill Company, 1966.
Basie, Count. *Good Morning Blues: The Autobiography of Count Basie, as told to Albert Murray.* New York: Random House, 1986.
Bechet, Sidney. *Treat It Gentle: An Autobiography.* New York: Hill and Wang, 1960.
Berendt, Joachim. *The Jazz Book.* New York: Lawrence Hill, 1975.
Berger, Morroe, Berger, Edward, and Patrick, James. *Benny Carter: A Life in American Music* (in two volumes). Metuchen, New Jersey: Scarecrow Press, 1982.
Blesh, Rudi and Janis, Harriet. *They All Played Ragtime.* New York: Oak Publications, 1971.

Charters, Samuel B. and Kunstadt, Leonard. *Jazz: A History of the New York Scene.* Garden City, New York: Doubleday, 1962.
Chilton, John. *Who's Who of Jazz.* Philadelphia: Chilton Book Company, 1972.
Connor, D. Russell and Hicks, Warren W. *BG on the Record: A Bio-discography of Benny Goodman.* New Rochelle, New York: Arlington House, 1969.

Dance, Stanley. *The World of Count Basie.* New York: Scribner's Sons, 1980.
____. *The World of Duke Ellington.* New York: Scribner's Sons, 1970.
____. *The World of Earl Hines.* New York: Scribner's Sons, 1977.
____. *The World of Swing.* New York: Scribner's Sons, 1974.
Delaunay, Charles (translated by Michael James). *Django Reinhardt.* London: Cassell, 1961.
Driggs, Frank and Lewine, Harris. *Black Beauty/White Heat: A Pictorial History of Classic Jazz.* New York: Morrow, 1982.

Ellington, Duke. *Music Is My Mistress.* Garden City, New York: Doubleday, 1973.
Ellington, Mercer and Dance, Stanley. *Duke Ellington in Person.* New York: Da Capo Press, 1979.
Ellison, Ralph. *Shadow and Act.* New York: Random House, 1964.
____. *Going to the Territory.* New York: Random House, 1986.

Feather, Leonard. *The Book of Jazz: A Guide From Then till Now.* New York: Horizon Press, 1965.
____. *The Encyclopedia of Jazz.* New York: Da Capo Press, 1984.

Gammond, Peter, ed. *Duke Ellington: His Life and Music.* New York: Da Capo Press, 1977.
Giddins, Gary. *Riding on a Blue Note.* New York: Oxford University Press, 1981.
____. *Rhythm-a-Ning.* New York: Oxford University Press, 1985.
Gillespie, Dizzy and Frazer, Al. *To Be or Not to Bop.* Garden City, New York: Doubleday, 1979.
Gitler, Ira. *Jazz Masters of the Forties.* New York: Macmillan Company, 1966.
____. *Swing to Bop.* New York: Oxford University Press, 1986.
Goldberg, Joe. *Jazz Masters of the Fifties.* New York: Macmillan Company, 1965.
Goodman, Benny and Kolodin, Irving. *The Kingdom of Swing.* New York: Stackpole Sons, 1939.

Hadlock, Richard. *Jazz Masters of the Twenties.* New York: Macmillan, 1965.
Handy, W.C., ed. *Blues: An Anthology.* New York: Da Capo Press, 1926.

Hentoff, Nat. *The Jazz Life.* New York: Da Capo Press, 1975.
Hentoff, Nat and Shapiro, Nat. *Hear Me Talkin' to Ya: An Oral History of Jazz.* New York: Dover Publications, 1966.
Hentoff, Nat and McCarthy, Albert, eds. *Jazz: New Perspectives on the History of Jazz.* New York: Da Capo Press, 1974.
Hodeir, André. *Jazz: Its Evolution and Essence.* New York: Da Capo Press, 1986.
——. *Toward Jazz.* New York: Da Capo Press, 1976.

Jepsen, Jorgen Grunnet. *Jazz Records: A Discography.* Holte, Denmark: K.E. Knudsen.
Jost, Ekkehard. *Free Jazz.* Graz: Universal Edition, 1974.

Keepnews, Orrin and Grauer, Bill. *A Pictorial History of Jazz.* New York: Crown Publishers, 1966.
Kirkeby, Ed. *Ain't Misbehavin': The Story of Fats Waller.* New York: Da Capo Press, 1975.

Litweiler, John. *The Freedom Principle.* New York: Morrow, 1984.

Meeker, David. *Jazz in the Movies.* New York: Da Capo Press, 1982.
Mellers, Wilfrid. *Music in a New Found Land.* New York: A.A. Knopf, 1965.
Merriam, Alan P. and Benford, Robert J. *A Bibliography of Jazz.* New York: Da Capo Press, 1970.
Mingus, Charles. *Beneath the Underdog.* New York: A.A. Knopf, 1971.
Murray, Albert. *The Omni-Americans.* New York: Outerbridge and Dienstfrey; distributed by E.P. Dutton, 1970.
——. *Stompin' The Blues.* New York: McGraw-Hill, 1976.

Pierson, Nathan. *Goin' to Kansas City.* Chicago, Illinois: University of Illinois Press, 1987.
Priestley, Brian. *Mingus: A Critical Biography.* New York: Da Capo Press, 1984.

Reisner, Robert. *Bird: The Legend of Charlie Parker.* New York: Da Capo Press, 1975, 1977.

Schuller, Gunther. *Early Jazz: Its Roots and Musical Development.* New York: Oxford University Press, 1968.
——. *Musings.* New York: Oxford University Press, 1986.
Simkins, C.O. *Coltrane: A Biography.* Herndon House, 1975.
Simosko, Vladimir and Tepperman, Barry. *Eric Dolphy: A Musical Biography and Discography.* New York: Da Capo Press, 1979.
Spellman, A.B. *Black Music: Four Lives in the Bebop Business.* New York: Schocken Books, 1970.
Stearns, Marshall Winslow. *Jazz Dance: The Story of American Vernacular Dance.* New York: Macmillan, 1968.
Stewart, Rex. *Jazz Masters of the Thirties.* New York: Da Capo Press, 1980, 1982.
Sudhalter, Richard M. *Bix: Man and Legend.* New Rochelle, New York: Arlington House, 1974.

Thomson, Virgil. *American Music Since 1910.* New York: Holt, Rinehart & Winston, 1971.

Ulanov, Barry. *Duke Ellington.* New York: Da Capo Press, 1975.

Williams, Martin. *Jazz Masters in Transition 1957–1969.* New York: Macmillan, 1970.
——. *Jazz Masters of New Orleans.* New York: Macmillan, 1967, 1978, 1979.
——. *The Jazz Tradition, New and Revised Edition.* New York: Oxford University Press, 1983.
——. *Where's The Melody?* New York: Pantheon Books, 1966, 1969.
——. *Jazz Heritage.* New York: Oxford University Press, 1985.
Wilson, John S. *Jazz: The Transition Years, 1940–1960.* New York: Appleton-Century-Crofts, 1966.

Discography

There are two standard discographical reference works, Brian Rust's *Jazz Records, 1897–1942,* two volumes, Arlington House, New Rochelle, NY 1978, and Jorgen Grunnet Jepsen's *Jazz Records, 1942–1967* (Write Walter C. Allen of Canada, Box 929, Adelaide Station, Toronto, Ontario M5C 2K3, Canada.)

Martin Williams, who also programmed and annotated *The Smithsonian Collection of Big Band Jazz* with Gunther Schuller, served for many years as director of the Smithsonian's jazz program. He is the author of several books on jazz, and his commentaries on jazz have appeared in the *Brittanica* and six other encyclopedias. He is now an acquisitions editor at the Smithsonian Institution Press.

Ira Gitler has been a professional observer of the jazz scene since the early 1950s. His most recent book is *Swing to Bop* (Oxford).